PERSPECTIVES ON ORGANIZATIONS

Viewpoints for Teachers

by

Ronald G. Corwin and Roy A. Edelfelt

Edited by

Theodore E. Andrews and Brenda L. Bryant

American Association of Colleges

for Teacher Education

and

Association of Teacher Educators, Washington, D.C.

ACKNOWLEDGMENTS

This book was produced by the Teacher Corps Networks under a grant from the United States Office of Education. The materials were prepared under Contract #300-75-0100 to the University of Nebraska from the United States Office of Education. The opinions expressed herein should not necessarily be construed as representing the opinions of the United States Office of Education.

Cover design by Studiofour Graphics

Technical Editing by Mary Gorman and Annette MacKinnon

Printed 1976 by
AMERICAN ASSOCIATION OF COLLEGES FOR TEACHER EDUCATION
Suite 610, One Dupont Circle, Washington, D.C. 20036

Printed in the United States of America

Library of Congress Catalog Card Number: 72-22919
Standard Book Number: 910052-98-0

CONTENTS

Editors and Contributors

Theodore E. Andrews, Director, Concern for Educational Development, Inc.

Brenda L. Bryant, Director, Concern for Educational Development, Inc.

Ronald G. Corwin, Professor of Sociology, The Ohio State University

Donald R. Cruickshank, Professor of Education, The Ohio State University

Roy A. Edelfelt, Professional Associate, Instruction and Professional Development, National Education Association

Dale Troxel, Program Director for Teacher Rights, Washington Education Association

Theodore Wagenaar, Assistant Professor of Sociology, Miami University, Oxford, Ohio

---

The opinions expressed herein should not necessarily be construed as representing the opinions of the agencies and institutions with which the editors and contributors are affiliated.

Foreword

This publication is one of many collaborative efforts undertaken over the years by the American Association of Colleges for Teacher Education and the Association of Teacher Educators. Our intent in publishing this document, in collaboration with Teacher Corps, U.S. Office of Education, is to provide ideas and information for those responsible for the preparation of education personnel. We believe that we can thus contribute to the improvement of educational opportunities for those who teach and learn in our schools.

Recent years have seen increasing efforts to meld the activities of the staffs of elementary-secondary schools with those of colleges and universities. This publication is useful to such personnel, for all need to study the operation of educational organizations. Pre- and in-service education personnel should know about organizations and be competent to perform effectively within them. We think that this document contributes to initial and continuing education of education personnel. In releasing this document, neither association necessarily endorses its contents. The purpose of our serving as publishers is to stimulate study and implementation of ideas and information as appropriate for local, state, and collegiate education agencies.

Creating a publication involves many individuals. We acknowledge with gratitude the efforts of the following: Ronald G. Corwin and Roy A. Edelfelt conceptualized and wrote much of the document. Theodore E. Andrews and Brenda Bryant did much substantive editing and writing to complete the manuscript. Joel L. Burdin and Florence Jones of AACTE carried out discussions which culminated in the final agreement for a cooperative publication venture. Technical editing was done by Annette MacKinnon of AACTE and Mary Gorman. Cover design is by Studiofour Graphics. None of the work could have been done without the encouragement and support of Teacher Corps Director William L. Smith, who over the years has done such an effective job in promoting American education.

Now, these efforts have reached their culmination in the release of *Perspectives on Organizations: Viewpoints for Teachers.* We believe that the usefulness of this document will justify the efforts which have made it possible.

Edward C. Pomeroy, Executive Director
American Association of Colleges for
Teacher Education

Robert J. Stevenson, Executive Director
Association of Teacher Educators

August 1976

Preface

The Teacher Corps conducted its first national training institute in the summer of 1975. New project interns and team leaders, called corps members, were participants in four intense weeks at the University of Richmond. In scope and content the institute was a unique response. Needs gave it birth; and evaluation studies, project directors, and research on the management of change gave it focus. The experience is known as the Corps Members Training Institute (CMTI).

The major impetus for the whole idea must be credited to third party program evaluations. More than one of these pointed up the great need for interns to understand the organizational features of schools. The Corwin Study in 1973 particularly described how crucial it was for our teaching teams, and particularly the interns, to understand the implications of organizational characteristics and realize that schools are social systems. The Marsh Study in 1974 reinforced this point.

Additionally, project directors were reporting that Teacher Corps interns needed an "esprit de corps," a personal identification with the national program effort. It also seemed to directors that a common training session could be the most realistic and profound cross-cultural learning and living experience ever provided by the Teacher Corps.

Finally, the research literature on the management of change and theories on the processes of change have important implications for teacher education. The Teacher Corps program is designed to help schools and colleges effect change. In the early history of the Corps, a basic assumption existed that interns, acting as change agents, could reform the school merely with their commitment and presence. This proved to be an unrealistic and unproductive assumption. We have now been careful to insist that Teacher Corps interns are not, and should not attempt to be, change agents. Our expectation is simply that they will be the best and most highly qualified teachers available to the profession, not in the traditional sense as dispensers of knowledge, but as facilitators of the learning process. This new role requires more and different theory and training than has been the case typically in teacher education. It starts with the assumption that facilitating means managing. Teachers must manage processes, products, and young people in an organized manner if they want and expect positive growth and change to occur in the learning and behavior of their students. This seems most accomplishable when the school is viewed as a formal organization, as a social system, and the classrooms in that school as subsystems. This systemic approach treats the classroom as an organization within an organization—the school.

Previous teacher training programs, which focused on the individual teacher learner, tended to provide new knowledge or skills to that teacher learner but did not have impact for change on the school to which the teacher returned. In many cases the teacher's new knowledge became a threat to teaching peers who had not themselves benefited from such training. Administrators were often threatened when the teacher attempted to implement this new knowledge and skill. We now know how these problems can be avoided. Many of us have come to believe that for the institutionalized growth and development of educational personnel, and for impact on the school, the school as an organization is the smallest unit of change. Similarly then, for the institutionalized growth and development of children, the classroom is the smallest unit of change.

Systems theory and organizational behavior theory have an important place in the conceptualization of preservice and inservice education. Many good and talented teachers feel unable to use their talents effectively because they believe the hierarchial structure of administrators, supervisors, and the environmental field force known as "the community" have placed unwarranted constraints upon them. This sense of alienation and powerlessness in the finest teachers will obviously prove contagious. Idealistic beginners will, therefore, hardly be immune. Teacher Corps is persuaded that if schools, as social systems, are to be changed for the better, everyone with a role or investment in the education and/or schooling of children must be collaboratively involved in the change process. If both new and experienced teachers were to have an opportunity to study the nature of organizations and the ways members interact, they might find that certain behavior characteristics manifested in schools are found in most organizations. Even more importantly, these behaviors can be understood and dealt with.

We know, of course, that most of the scientific data on organization are found in studies of economic and industrial organizations. Over the past few years, universities have conducted numerous educational organization studies in educational administration for middle managers and school superintendents, initially supported through the Kellogg Foundation Program. No one, it seemed, had begun to develop concepts, theoretical formulations, and case studies for prospective and practising teachers to use in studying the school as a formal organization. With the exception of the initial work on organization study done by Chris Argyris for employees, little else had been developed for a role group below that of administrators and managers. Someone somewhere had to begin.

The Corps Member Training Institute was seen as having three goals. The first was to develop an esprit de corps among our newest members. The second was to provide them with a rich multicultural experience. The third was to involve them and their experienced teacher team leader in an academic experience designed to open their eyes to theories of organization, both structure and behavior, and to the many styles of learning and teaching there are. The Institute was organized into the two separate graduate-level strands, Organization Perspectives, and Teaching and Learning Style Analysis. This volume is the first of a series which deals with Perspectives on Organizations.

It would be impossible to name everyone who contributed to the Corps Member Training Institute, but some cannot go without mention. We must acknowledge the people who had undue pressures on them to conceive, develop, and implement the entire project in so short a time, and who amazingly did it. Ron Corwin and Roy Edelfelt were responsible for this organization strand; Dale Lake and Matt Miles served as design consultants; Jack Gant, Emily Feistritzer, Elaine Witty, Theodore Andrews, and Larry Iannoccone, as cluster leaders, brought reality and reason out of the rhetoric.

It will become obvious to the reader that nothing of the Teaching and Learning Style Analysis Strand is included in this volume. It was a separate unit with an almost entirely different staff, different teaching philosophy, and different training materials. These materials will be available at a later date. Bruce Joyce and his associates, Marsha Weil and Michael McKibben, were responsible for this teaching and learning strand.

Dean Floyd Waterman and Associate Deans Bambi Cardenas, Roger W. Wilson, and Vergia Gambrill were responsible for the administrative and logistical details during the four week CMTI. All of these people mentioned above have the gratitude of all who were a part of the Richmond learning community adventure.

Its outcome, as revealed so far by the Interim Report of the G. Thomas Fox Evaluation, has been truly impressive. That document leaves little doubt that the instructional process used at Richmond did develop a sense of community. The multicultural interactions were rich, and a real esprit de corps emerged. It is also apparent that many previous assumptions about teaching and internship were challenged. Changes in perspective did take place. Although the follow-up study should tell us more about the impact of the four weeks, the results already reported have more than confirmed their value.

The Teacher Corps is pleased to have the American Association of Colleges for Teacher Education and the Association of Teacher Educators serve as joint publishers of this volume. Their constituencies are important ones in any effort to implement change in the preparation of education personnel. Their effort is to provide practitioners, decision makers, and researchers with the ideas and information which can become building steps to progress.

This volume offers those who may share our concerns some of the papers, other materials, and procedures that were used to give corpsmembers a new perspective on organizations. Much of the value of these materials was the extent to which they generated debate and interaction, both of which were encouraged by a group of talented instructors.

They are presented as beginnings, at least, of a response to a serious need. The two subsequent volumes on *Perspectives on Organizations* will focus on other aspects of the CMTI. Each reinforces the single fact that systems and organization theory are no luxury items in a realistic program of teacher training.

> *William L. Smith*
> *Director*
> *Teacher Corps*
>
> *August 1976*

Introduction

Perspectives on Organizations is a series of training publications designed to develop among future and practicing teachers an awareness of what organizations are, how organizations affect them, and how they can deal with organizations. The materials in this series were developed when Teacher Corps decided to include the study of organizations in its 1975 Corps Member Training Institute for preservice and inservice teachers. At the invitation of William L. Smith, director of Teacher Corps, we began to plan and develop the procedures and materials to be used during the institute's component on the study of organizations. With Teacher Corps' support we were responsible for planning the instructional mode, for selecting instructional materials, and for initiating the development of new materials which focus especially on the unique concerns new and experienced teachers encounter in their roles in the organizations.

So often, new areas of study are initiated independently, by an academician or by practitioners. However, we worked cooperatively to create this new emphasis for teacher training. This is not just another case of "applied social science," where a scholar is called upon to apply technical skills to a problem defined by others, or to lead an investigation. Nor is it a case of a practitioner acquainting a naive social scientist with the facts of life. From the beginning, this has been a joint venture between a teacher educator (Edelfelt) and a sociologist (Corwin). We have learned from one another, and we have learned together. It is our hope, indeed our conviction, that this type of collaborative effort can be successful for others as well. The concerns of teacher education and of sociology are too intimately linked to remain divorced in separate traditions.

The materials and activities in this volume were designed and selected by us, and compiled, edited, and prepared for publication by Theodore E. Andrews and Brenda L. Bryant, both of whom were instructors in the Corps Member Training Institute in 1975. James P. Steffensen, Teacher Corps, reviewed the materials and worked closely with the publication's editors.

Viewpoints for Teachers is the first volume in the series *Perspectives on Organizations.* The Preface, by William L. Smith, underscores the significant contribution the study of organizations can make to the field of teacher education. Part I, "Teaching and Learning About Organizations," contains an overview, rationale for the study, and instructional objectives. Part II, "Life in Organizations," is an introduction to organization theory and basic related concepts. Divided into two sections, Part II provides the content for *Viewpoints for Teachers.* The subject of Part III, "Organizations in Action," tells how the instructors and learners might go about exploring organizational concepts. Activities explained in Part III can be used to enrich the examination of key concepts and to draw on the experience of participants as a critical element of learning. The "Vignettes" in Part III were contributed by Donald Cruickshank, professor of education at The Ohio State University. An annotated bibliography by Theodore C. Wagenaar, a sociologist at Miami University, appears as Appendix A.

It is difficult to capture in print the enthusiasm that users of these materials have expressed during their study of organizations. However, a sense of their mood is reflected in excerpts from participants' comments, quoted in Part I. The ultimate value that comes

1

from a sharpened awareness of organizations, of course, can be assessed better at a later time. Some of our own faith in this range potential is expressed in the following entry from a journal kept by a Teacher Corps intern:

> A sincere and relevant evaluation of the study of organizations can be made only at a later date. Its impact will be evident only as I encounter school organizations face-to-face. When I am actively part of the school system, when I enter an organizational conflict and attempt to effect some manner of change, I will look behind me then and say, "That's where I was." And by knowing where I was, I will know where I am.

Helping readers better understand "where I am" and the options they have in deciding "where I want to be" is a basic purpose of *Perspectives on Organizations.*

Roy Edelfelt
and
Ronald Corwin

Part I

Teaching and Learning about Organizations

RATIONALE

The purpose of **Perspectives on Organizations** is to help prospective and practicing teachers become more aware of the major characteristics of organizations, and the problems that result from or are aggravated by these characteristics. A glance through the Yellow Pages of any telephone directory will suggest that there are nearly as many organizations as there are people. We all have contact with many organizations each day; grocery stores, fraternities, corporations, employee groups, churches, hospitals, and schools.

Usually, organizations are established to perform specified functions for society. Their purpose is to provide greater efficiency and coordination in particular areas than individuals alone can achieve. However, organizations vary greatly in effectiveness, goals, forms of control, members, and in the beneficiaries of their services or products. Some have become highly complex, others remain simple.

Out of necessity, all of us have adopted some assumptions about organizations as we try to understand, predict, control, or otherwise cope with the problems that we often encounter in our organizational roles. However, we all could profit from an opportunity to sharpen our awareness of how organizations operate and to reexamine our assumptions about them. Such knowledge can help us understand our roles in organizations, our influence on organizations, and their impact on us. Sometimes, it can help us avoid being the victims of organizations. Moreover, if an individual aspires to change or improve an organization, being able to analyze how it works can assist immeasurably in influencing its direction, purpose, and procedures. At the same time, some study and reflection will make it clear that the process of organizational change is complex — so complex that normally a given individual can play only a relatively modest part in it.

Unfortunately, teachers have had almost no formal training in the complexities of organizations. And yet, perhaps more than other professionals, they must deal with numerous organizations in the practice of their profession. In addition, they must function effectively as members of several key organizations — the school, the school system, and the teacher organization. They play different roles in these organizations — as professional employees of the school district, members of a staff hierarchy, and members of teacher organizations — and the expectations associated with each of these roles are often in conflict, posing hard professional choices for teachers. Moreover, these roles typically have low status in the respective hierarchies; for example, although teachers are autonomous in certain respects, they are relatively powerless as individuals to control the key decisions that are made in a school. Collectively, however, teachers are effecting changes. Teacher organizations, such as the National Education Association (NEA) and the American Federation of Teachers (AFT), have exerted considerable power in the last decade.

Multiple memberships, status problems, and role conflicts are not unique to teachers;

3

they are common aspects of life in organizations. Teachers can better understand these aspects in relation to other organizational phenomena and characteristics, by studying the structure and various patterns of behavior in organizations, that is, discrepancies between power and authority, boundary defenses, recruitment and evaluation, organizational change, relations with outside groups, etc. For example, it should be useful for teachers to reflect on what typically happens as organizations become larger — employees become more specialized, their autonomy increases, and there is greater likelihood of conflict. Better understanding can also be achieved by a comparative study of organizations; for example, by comparing human service organizations to organizations with more concrete products, and by comparing school organizations to other human service groups.

Belief that the study of organizations would benefit teachers was reaffirmed in a major, three-year longitudinal study of the Teacher Corps.* One significant finding of that study was that those teacher interns bent on reform in schools were "relatively ineffective" because they violated many norms of the existing school system. They failed, not because they couldn't teach students, but because they violated established customs and rules of the organization. Corwin concludes that:

> Although doomed to frustration, they (interns) provided a thrust for change. But these questions arise: Is it possible to train people who are passionately committed to the need for reform and who are calculating and patient enough to work effectively within the system? Can they become sophisticated about the system without losing their zest for change? Can they learn to temper their romanticism without losing their compassion for and optimism concerning the children?*

William Smith, director of Teacher Corps, recognized the significance and validity of these questions, and through his efforts a training program for Teacher Corps interns devoted to the study of organizations was developed. This effort, the Corps Member Training Institute held in the summer of 1975 at the University of Richmond, provided the impetus for publication of this series of training materials devoted to the study of organizations.

The content and procedures included in this and subsequent volumes were developed to assist persons in building training programs that would sharpen awareness and develop skills in dealing with organizations. Many of the materials and procedures included were successfully used in the Teacher Corps Institute.

Success ultimately depends on how teachers actually function in schools and communities, and there has not been sufficient time to assess this. There is, however, evidence of learning in the journals, daily records of personal reactions, kept by interns and team leaders (experienced teachers) during the Institute. The excerpts from journals illustrate how the participants felt during the two-week, full-time Institute. Participants, all college graduates, were prospective and experienced teachers.

Participant Awareness of Goals

Goals of the study of organizations are to develop an awareness of characteristics of organizations and an understanding of how organizational phenomena impinge on teachers in the school and community. Awareness was verbalized in various ways by participants. Among them was a recognition of realism:

---

*R. G. Corwin, **Reform and Organizational Survival: The Teacher Corps as an Instrument of Organizational Change** (New York: Wiley-Interscience, 1973), p. 375.

I came into the teaching field idealistic, hopeful, and committed to being a part of the change. Now, I, too, hope to derive or effect "reasonable expectations" and a hardheaded realistic approach to problems.

or of complexity:

I wasn't aware of all that is involved in an organization. So many things we've talked about in groups I've known but taken for granted, never asked why.

or the importance of analysis:

Today I finally saw how studying organizations will help me when I return to the community where I will work. I think I can better analyze situations and see things from all perspectives.

One participant admits that organizations sound dull:

My initial feelings were "Oh, boy — organizations. It sounds dull."
All and all, these past two weeks have been anything but dull. About one week into the course my brain began to pull things together; and the papers, speakers, movies, and experiences of others began to be integrated into my own past, present, and future. At this point I feel that I have enough knowledge about organizations to be confident in my future.

This shows an awareness that some things are inevitable. For another participant that realization had a very practical value:

Organizations are a fact of life. Since we all must deal with many different types, we should know how they are structured so we will have that information when we need it. If we don't understand our own organization and our position in it, we may lose our jobs because of things beyond our control.

Others, perhaps more optimistic, saw possibilities for individual choices but recognized the importance of thoughtful and considered decisions:

We have read, heard, and spoken about many different options in dealing with organizations. All offered us one basic notion. Options for dealing with organizations are there for us to discover.
I have learned an awful lot, a great deal more than I now can appreciate. The most prominent thing is that I have not recognized organizations and their characteristics in many instances.

Awareness of organizations also generated some rejection and fear:

I have realized for the first time that I do not like organizations. I've never thought of it in this way — I've reacted against an oppressive high school, avoided large, rigid classes at college, worked exclusively with small business (construction, farm work, informal restaurants) — but I have never thought of my behavior as a reaction against organizations in general, and now I feel certain that it is. The most frightening thing for me about getting involved in schools is that I could become the victim of the organization, or worse yet, that I may become insensitive to human needs and perpetuate the system.

And fear included apprehensions about the power of knowledge:

I believe that knowledge corrupts, especially knowledge like this which gives us so much insight into organizations, power, and authority. I have never taken courses that I felt would aid me in coercing people. I strongly believe in letting people think their own thoughts. I am a little afraid of the potential of this new knowledge. I hope that I will put the new knowledge to good use.

Still another participant saw the prospect of changing the system and not becoming the victim of an organization:

I have gained a clearer appreciation of the complexity of organizations and realize that effective change involves understanding the power structure and interactions within and outside the organization. I'm beginning to see how organizations shape the behavior of individuals and the reasons for such behavior. I'm not so quick to condemn the organization, nor am I blindly accepting the status quo as being absolute. The potential for the organization to absorb the individual is great, but an individual has the ability to maintain freedom and integrity if he or she understands how organizations function. The individual can continue to be free and make needed changes within the system. Through persistence and hard work, I still believe organizations can be made more humane and responsive to the needs of the people they are supposed to serve.

The study of organizations is also designed to build an information base and professional sophistication. There were many journal entries that illustrated that kind of achievement. When students can verbalize the knowledge they have acquired, the first step in behavioral change may have taken place. The following are a few of the unsolicited recordings of ideas, information, and facts that participants thought significant enough to write down:

I feel that it is extremely important that a teacher know his or her rights, because the organization will not keep him informed of them for obvious reasons.

* * *

I learned today that being a member of several organizations often causes a conflict in roles between the organizations.

* * *

It's OK to be a puppet in an organization for a period of time until one builds a power base from within and/or without so that one can promote whatever is necessary.

* * *

To effect change at a particular level within an organization, one must effect an involvement from the level above that level needing change.

* * *

Organizations do **not** have to have specific goals as some theorists believe. Instead, they may have conflicting goals on several levels of the organization, changing goals, or lost goals.

* * *

Teachers are closest to students in the school hierarchy and should be in the best position to understand their needs, desires, and problems. But despite this, teachers are in the toughest position (besides students) to implement change.

* * *

Obviously, process and content were highly integrated, and this blend is recommended for anyone using these materials.

The content-process mix is illustrated in the use of selected feature films. Participants reacted to this approach:

> At first, I resented having to watch the movie, but when I saw it, I saw the relevance and was able to apply it to organization theory and what we had discussed about organizations that morning.

* * *

> Monday night we saw the movie "Bridge on the River Kwai." I enjoyed looking at it from the organizational perspective. After the movie a group of friends discussed the questions, and I got a lot from it.
> In the morning we went to our cluster meeting to discuss the movie. The conflict between **authority and technical skills** brought out the concept that different cultures and organizations have different rules and characteristics, norms and sanctions. There are different bases for authority, leadership, rank, and technical skills, and in order to have an effective powerful organization, there must be expertise in any of those.

Case studies were used in conjunction with films and other written materials to stimulate thought and discussion. The effect of the multifaceted approach is illustrated by another participant, as follows:

> In the afternoon we did a case study which made me see how organizational norms and characteristics come in conflict and how organizational goals limit personal freedom. I tried to relate those thoughts to the movie and once more was somehow uncomfortable with the idea of having to sacrifice personal individual freedom in order to survive in an organization.

The instructional setting can also be analyzed and studied where possible, as one example of an organization. Suggestions for a mode of instruction, which the authors and editors of these materials have used and strongly endorse, are included in Part II, Section 2, What Are Organizations Like?.

Participant reactions supported our initial ideas:

> The last two weeks have been meaningful. This is the first time that I have been with a group of people of all races, colors, and creeds interacting together.

* * *

> Before coming to this institute I didn't express myself verbally in groups, but I thank this experience for helping me to open up and express myself in groups. The uneasy feeling is gone.

* * *

> Meeting and talking with people of different backgrounds, both educationally and culturally, is probably one of the best learning experiences.

* * *

> I feel comfortable with my group, my cluster, with the whole organization. This is unusual for me. I don't make friends easily.

* * *

> Without a doubt the most beneficial part of these first two weeks has been the opportunity to interact with people from many different ethnic backgrounds. I'm surprised at the

number of informal discussions I've been in in which the topic of organizations has been debated, argued, and thrashed about.

An experienced teacher reacts:

> It is very important to interact with other people and to really discuss these concepts. I can honestly say that I learned many characteristics, concepts, and definitions of organizational theory. I have taken many administration and supervision courses where organizational theory was dealt with, but I have never grasped the concepts as well as I have here. I think that this is due mainly to the small group activities we have had. My experience has always been a lecture kind of situation where we never had much opportunity to discuss and interact with the people in the class. Some of the activities we had were very effective in that we were actually experiencing processes of organizational theory. For example, we got into triads to answer questions, and in another activity we had to put ourselves in a principal's position and become the helpee.

A final reaction epitomizes the conviction of many participants and all the staff involved in the Institute and reiterates a continuing, nagging question of all teachers and students: Will I apply what I have learned?

> A sincere and relevant evaluation of the study of organizations can be made only at a later date. Its impact will be evident only as I encounter school organizations face-to-face. When I am actively part of the school system, when I enter an organizational conflict and attempt to effect some manner of change, I will look behind me then and say, "That's where I was." And by knowing where I was, I will know where I am.

INSTRUCTIONAL MODE

The instructional mode used during the Corps Member Training Institute was important in ensuring the effectiveness of the materials and the favorable responses of participants. Suggestions for the mode and tone of instruction follow:

1. *Instruction should occur in small groups.* Ideally participants should be organized in basic discussion groups of about 10 members with one instructor for each group. Diversity of background among group members and instructors is highly desirable. Instructors should be flexible and vary the program to meet the demands of an evolving instructional process.

2. *Instruction should give attention to the needs and interests of participants.* The backgrounds and levels of sophistication of participants should be assessed prior to, or at the first meeting, so that planning and grouping is responsive to the diversity and needs of participants.

3. *Instructional expectations should be made public.* Participants should receive statements of training goals and objectives, how those goals and objectives will be achieved, and indicators of how the participants will be evaluated.

4. *Instruction should provide for intensive involvement of participants.* Special effort should be made to select case studies, papers, vignettes, readings, abstracts, and films that are particularly suited to participants who are preservice or inservice teachers. Small group discussion should be planned to give every participant an active part in establishing a rationale, making choices and decisions, and testing principles and theories inherent in different kinds of organizations.

5. *Instruction should capitalize on the temporary society created by the group itself.* Characteristics of the group, as illustrated in its governance and its social and work problems, may be used for analysis and diagnosis, providing a real situation with which individuals and groups can deal.

6. *Instruction should deal with process problems and skills as part of instruction.* How and why people behave in certain ways in an organization is part of learning about organizations. As appropriate, participants should use illustrations of their own behavior to analyze why particular progress or achievement by a group has or has not been made.

7. *Instruction should engage participants directly with problems of analysis, diagnosis, and choice.* In part, this point reiterates numbers 4 and 5. In addition, participants should have instructors and speakers interrogate and discuss field experiences, role playing situations, and other experiences. In all of these activities, the purpose is to deal directly and personally with how effectively one can work through a problem in a logical, rational way.

8. *Instruction should provide a variety of activities.* Engaging the interest of people in studying organizations is not easy. A variety of activities enriches the training session; for example, case studies, film and vignette analysis, field-based study of various organizations, independent study, readings, and films which are appropriate for use in groups of various sizes.

9. *Instruction should include close guidance, monitoring, and evaluation of participants.* The instructor-participant ratio should allow some one-to-one contact, providing opportunities to discuss how the goals of the program fit those of the individual and to negotiate modifications when possible. Such modifications, of course, become a matter of record and provide some data for program evaluation. The instructor's responsibility for evaluation is continuous and should be done cooperatively with participants.

10. *Instruction should respect the status of all participants.* Although all participants (and instructors as well) are learners, each participant presumably has a different status based on his or her competence, experience, and power position. This is especially true if a group contains both preservice and inservice teachers. Each person's place in the hierarchy should be recognized and respected.

We recognize that these 10 points are appropriate to study in any field and all to often are unattainable for one or more reasons. Yet, a large part of the success of the Corps Member Training Institute was attributable to a continuous effort to follow these principles. Each person using this material for instructional purposes will need to decide how best to present the concepts based on ever changing tradeoffs among the instructors' skills, the learners' needs, and the administrative support systems.

GOALS AND OBJECTIVES

The instructional setting described above and the materials contained in Parts II and III of this book work together, enabling participants to achieve certain goals and objectives. The goals and objectives are shared with participants so that everyone is aware of the purposes for studying organizations.

The overall goal of *Perspectives on Organizations* is to:

- Develop an awareness of the characteristics and functions of organizations, and of how organizations and individuals influence each other.

The program designed to help participants reach this goal includes instruction to:

- Enable participants to identify problems that result from or are aggravated by some characteristics of organizations.
- Provide participants with skills, enabling them to analyze organizations and organizational problems.
- Build participant interest in continuing independent study of organizations in the future.

When they have completed the program, participants should be able to demonstrate (through analysis and discussion of organizations) that they have:

- An understanding of why it is important to study organizations.
- A knowledge of some of the complexities resulting from membership in organizations.
- The ability to define organizations, social systems, bureaucracy, organization theory.
- An awareness of approaches used to study organizations.
- An awareness of some key features of organizations.
- An understanding of how the various functions of organizations are coordinated.
- An awareness of models that are useful for analyzing organizations.
- The ability to classify organizations according to typology.
- An understanding of how the social environment might affect the organization.
- A knowledge of strategies for coping in organizations.

These, and perhaps other objectives that participants will identify for themselves, should be achieved as study proceeds. Participants and instructors will frequently want to refer back to these objectives to assess progress. The materials and activities designed to help achieve the objectives are contained in Parts II and III.

Part II

Life in Organizations

Life in Organizations was written by Ronald G. Corwin and Roy A. Edelfelt. Oriented to prospective and practicing teachers, it provides a general overview for the study of organizations. The major concepts discussed in this part are listed in the chart at the beginning of Part III.

This part is divided into two sections to aid participants and instructors in their reading and discussion. The first section, "Why Study Organizations?", contains a rationale for the study of organizations by teachers and others, some definitions, and an introduction to theories of and approaches to the study of organizations. The second section, "What Are Organizations Like?", provides further, more detailed information useful for analyzing organizations.

Participants and instructors may find it helpful to read and reread this part of the book as they work through the activities contained in Part III. As terms and concepts appear in the various activities, the reader will find *Life in Organizations* a helpful reference. The paragraphs are numbered and the concepts contained in those paragraphs are keyed to each of the instructional activities. (See activities list on first page of Part III.) Participants and instructors are encouraged to use these and other activities they will develop to examine the contents of Part II in depth.

Section 1: Why Study Organizations?

Roy A. Edelfelt   Ronald G. Corwin

WHO STUDIES ORGANIZATIONS?

Much has been written about organizations, but authors usually either take a detached view or address themselves to administrators or people in positions of authority (Haas and Drabeck, 1973; Lane, Corwin, and Monahan, 1967). Consequently, scholars have been preoccupied either with abstract theories or with problems of management and supervision. They seldom have written for lower echelon people like factory workers, clerks, teachers, or social workers. The reasons are understandable: consultant-writers are usually hired by administrators, and most college courses on this subject serve administrative training programs, while the few remaining courses are offered in academic departments with no special allegiances. As a result, administrators probably have an advantage over employees. We find this situation ironic. For, as one of the first social

1*

---

*Certain paragraphs are numbered for use with the chart in Part III, p. 47.

scientists to call attention to the oversight has concluded (Argyris, 1957), most human problems in organizations inadvertently arise because of the way work roles have been designed for people in subordinate positions. In addition to this practical need to solve some human problems, which Argyris has stressed, there has been a trend toward the democratic action of organizations, which also requires employees to become more sophisticated about organizations. We sense that lower echelon professionals are beginning to recognize that organization theory can be as useful to them as to their employers. Indeed, many progressive administrators may prefer workers who are capable of making more informed judgments about their organizations.

2 In sum, we are convinced that if the study of organizations is worthy and useful enough to be included in training programs for administrators of businesses, hospitals, and school systems, it certainly also ought to be helpful to all members of organizations.

3 Of course, each of us encounters many organizations as citizens as well as employees. We can all profit from learning to deal more effectively with organizations such as banks, restaurants, department stores, national food chains, churches, welfare agencies, tennis clubs, funeral homes, and jails, as well as our places of work. Much of our lifestyle, including even our recreation, depends on how we are treated by members of these organizations and, in turn, how we deal with them. So, we shall raise some questions, not with the primary intention of providing the answers, but with the hope of building awareness and arousing interest and the desire to deal more deliberately with organizations. But first, let us confront a basic issue.

WHY STUDY ORGANIZATIONS?

4 Because each of us belongs to many organizations, is it reasonable to assume that we already know enough about them? What can further study add to what we have learned from experience? Do knowledge and theory of organizations have anything to offer beyond translating what we know into jargon? These are fair questions. We are all assaulted by knowledge. Hucksters—professors, teachers, librarians, and advertisers—try to convince us that unless we assimilate the subject they are pushing, we will deprive ourselves of lasting beauty, fun, wisdom, or worse, income. So unless one is convinced that it is at least as important to understand organizations as it is to understand baseball, banking investment, growing roses, a foreign language, or our heritage, it isn't worth proceeding.

5 Let us think about it. In the following discussion we shall try to identify at least three related reasons why studying organizations might be of some use.

The AHA! Feeling: The First Reason for Studying Organizations

6 First, let us start by assuming that organizations are a basic part of everyone's existence. The problems they frequently pose for individuals have been dramatized in modern novels, in which the hero is often portrayed as an employee. The dilemma posed in Herman Wouk's *The Caine Mutiny* (1951) is typical: the employee ought to have the right to his own integrity, but bureaucracy erodes his responsibility and compromises his moral integrity.

7 But even if we did not have to cope daily with dozens of organizations, they would be relevant to our lives in the way that the stars are relevant—as part of our social universe, they shape our perspectives. Whether one is a teacher, nurse, salesperson, or factory worker, to be fully effective one must first be an interesting person with a broad perspective and an awareness of the surrounding world.

12

Perhaps because organizations are so familiar to us, we are often tempted to dismiss all but the most practical information about them as irrelevant. We probably would not dream of demanding quite the same degree of relevance or practicality when we study art, literature, or many other scientific fields. For most "practical" purposes, what difference does it make whether or not the earth is the center of the universe?. . .whether the world is flat, or round?. . .whether there is a law of gravity, or not? For centuries, people were able to get along using faulty assumptions about these matters. And yet in a larger, philosophical sense, each discovery of a new truth has been mind-shattering. We have learned that we, as human beings, are not the center of the universe; and although this awareness has created an identity crisis, it has also forced us to think differently of ourselves and our world. 8

We doubt that the study of organizations has yet produced so dramatic a breakthrough in perspective; but we are convinced that if we were to view organizations with the same detachment as scientists have viewed astronomy, biology, or geography, our perspectives on the world would be enlarged and immensely enriched. Perhaps we can illustrate. Many people seem to start with the assumption that organizations are no more than groups of people, and, therefore, people are the sources of the problems. For instance, when lower-class children are mistreated in schools, it is popular to place the blame on the personal biases of "middle-class teachers." But that is too simple. People's attitudes and actions are also shaped by the organizations they belong to, that is, by the demands and circumstances of their jobs. Many of the problems in low-income schools arise because of the fact that many *organizational norms*—such as punctuality, dependability, respect for people in authority, nonagression, and the like—conflict with the life-styles of many lower-class children (Corwin, 1965). Replacing the teachers might help, but it would not solve the basic problem. By the same token, teachers cannot take full credit when people are treated fairly, because practices—such as merit examinations, promotion on the basis of competence or seniority, objectivity, and the like—have evolved in the name of efficiency as well as democracy. The way people behave is often determined by the criteria used to evaluate them. If prejudiced teachers are likely to be fired for expressing their beliefs, they will be less likely to express those beliefs. Similarly, if a public high school program is judged on how many graduates are admitted to college, teachers and administrators will probably spend more time with children in the college curriculum than with those in the vocational program. 9

To develop a broad perspective, knowledge is needed about many types of organizations (Heydebrand, 1973). There are several reasons for saying this. One is that each of us belongs to many types of organizations, and we will join still other organizations in the future. Even if one is preparing for a specific vocation, such as social worker, teacher, or nurse, eventually one may leave this job to go into administration, private practice, or another career. It would therefore be shortsighted to concentrate too narrowly on any particular type of job or organization. 10

We believe studying a variety of organizations will help us gain perspective and become more aware of the many ways in which they can be organized. Sometimes the solutions that have been found in one type of organization can be adapted to others. People who are preoccupied with only one type of organization miss the breadth of perspective that comes from a comparative approach. We tend to take for granted the characteristics of the organization that we are familiar with; we view them as givens rather than as variables that might be altered to achieve different effects. For example, in most public schools, teachers do not have much choice in the students assigned to them; nor do stu- 11 dents choose the teachers to whom they are assigned. This system of arbitrary assignments has been largely taken for granted. But why is this practice so common? What would happen if the system were changed, if students could openly negotiate for their teachers, and teachers for their students? We seldom ask such questions. (A few schools are experimenting along these lines.)

The Practical Value of Impractical Knowledge:
A Second Reason for Studying Organizations

12   The study of organizations can also be useful in providing perspective. Basic knowledge and understanding can be likened to financial capital, there to be drawn upon as the need arises, even if we are not sure how it will be used. Basic knowledge can be adapted for a variety of unforeseen circumstances, and for this reason, it is ultimately more useful to an adept person than more immediately useful information, such as prescriptions for coping with specific, very restricted types of problems.

13   Each of us has ideas about how organizations operate, based on the "street knowledge" of personal experiences. We have tried to cash a check on an out-of-town bank, or tried to register at a hotel when the clerk has no record of the reservation, or tried to qualify for a welfare service, or tried to locate a medical specialist familiar with a unique medical problem. When we confront these kinds of problems, we are forced to use some "theory" about how the organization operates in order to deal with it. So the question is not whether theories of organizations are *useful*; we use them every day. The question is whether we can improve our theories by studying and thinking about organizations.

14   Sometimes our conclusions turn out to be very simple, if not naive. For example, the clerk is a fool or worse, a psychopath; the manager takes bribes; the organization responds only to force (or shouting); or the customer has no recourse but to accept his or her fate. We have talked with people who seem to have some rather shortsighted views about how organizations operate. For example, one school teacher we talked with was asked to identify the source of some of the problems in her school. She said that was not difficult; all of them could be attributed to the principal. He was enforcing some rules too rigidly, like the times teachers should be in the building, restrictions concerning noise in the building, and students in the hallways during classes. He refused to modify decisions regarding the assignment of aides to teachers and the assignment of teachers to patrol or hall duty. As we talked, however, it became evident that the principal was responding to pressures from the superintendent's office and from a group of citizens over whom he had little control. Furthermore, there were no formal channels through which the teacher could communicate the seriousness of her individual concerns, and for a variety of reasons, she did not try to use collective power. Even if the principal had been replaced, it probably would not have made much difference in this situation. Yet that was essentially this teacher's only proposal. Of course, some individuals are already more sophisticated about organizations than others; so there is no simple starting point, except to assume that each of us probably can benefit by sharing the wisdom of others.

Helpful Hints to Almost Anyone:
A Third Reason for Studying Organizations

15   Realistically, of course, we know that for some people neither philosophical merit nor long-range utility is enough to justify taking time to study organizations. We also have an argument for those people. Employees often lose their jobs, or get passed over at

promotion time, because they do not fully understand their organization. School teaching is a good example. Teachers more frequently lose their jobs because they fail to conform to or deal with certain rules, such as being punctual, keeping accurate records, maintaining discipline, or getting along with the administration and the parents, than because they are incompetent as teachers of a particular area of study.

We do not mean to imply that employees should merely conform. An individual has [16] the right, sometimes the obligation, to take issue, even to deliberately choose to sacrifice a job rather than give up his or her own personal values. However, we believe that in many cases people make poor choices unnecessarily; there are often alternatives that could have been chosen if the situation had been fully analyzed.

Most training programs ignore the development of organizational skills and stress [17] only the limited technical skills related to the job. Because the full social context in which trainees eventually will work is ignored, novices often experience a "reality shock" soon after they take their first job (Corwin, Taves, and Haas, 1961). They become disillusioned with their training because it did not provide guidance in helping them to cope with, or even anticipate, inconsistent demands they encountered.

We believe that new, and even experienced, teachers could use this kind of help. [18] But some of the teachers we have talked with are not so sure. Their primary satisfactions come from working with children in the classroom or from their subject-matter specialty. In the classroom with the door shut the rest of the school system seems remote, if not actually irrelevant. So why think about the larger system? Only what goes on in the classroom is important. Or so it seems. But this attitude is ultimately unrealistic. Teachers must be different with different people. In fact, to operate as a fully functioning professional, the teacher must assume several roles; teaching students is just one of them. In addition to being the teacher of students, the teacher is also a member of a faculty, a member of a staff hierarchy, a liaison with parents and the community, a member of a teacher organization, and a member of the teaching profession.

Legitimizing at least these roles seems essential if the teacher is to qualify as a pro- [19] fessional worker. All these roles contribute in some way, directly or indirectly, to the central function of teaching: helping students learn. But they also have professional and organizational dimensions distinct from the role of teacher of students. For example, in the teacher's role as a member of a staff hierarchy, there are relationships with subordinates that must be managed smoothly and effectively; the teacher is on the one hand a manager or leader of teacher aides, clerks, and other support staff, but he or she is also dependent on the direction and decisions of a principal and superintendent. At the same time that the teacher deals with a hierarchical administrative relationship, he or she must also carry on professional interaction, as a particular kind of expert, which requires quite different relationships with peers and other levels of the hierarchy.

In addition to understanding individual roles in the organization, the individual needs [20] to understand that the organization may provide protection. How far can the teacher go in the classroom without the aid of the larger organization? Teachers have traditionally relied on the principal or other administrators to defend them from a variety of pressures and influences, such as the criticisms of parents seeking to switch Johnny to another teacher, to have his grade revised, or to get him in the school play. And when all else fails, the unruly child can be expelled. Even the most independent teacher relies on assistance from a team of people—peers, subordinates, and superordinates—such as reading specialists, counselors, aides, student teachers, the school secretary, and the custodians. Increasingly, when problems in teaching stem from the larger system, teachers are relying on their teachers' organization to protect them.

21   These claims may seem exaggerated. We are not, of course, promising that knowing about organizations is a panacea, that it guarantees doing a better job. There is no guarantee, and we are suspicious of such claims. But knowledge about organizations will not hurt either. And it might help.

DOES A PERSON HAVE ANY ALTERNATIVE TO BECOMING PART OF ORGANIZATIONS?

The Robinson Crusoe Dream

22   In one sense everyone must become part of organizations, and hence must "conform." But the answer is obviously more complicated than that. In the first place, there are some alternatives to being a member of a large-scale organization. One might go into small business, farming, private consulting, tutoring, arts and crafts, etc. However, there are relatively few occupations like this, so most of us will end up as employees of large organizations. Moreoever, even people in these independent occupations often affiliate among themselves in trade associations, professional organizations, cooperatives, and the like, and in any event, they must deal with large-scale organizations which supply materials, buy their products, license them, handle advertising or legal problems, and so on. (This of course does not mean that the problems of coping with an organization are the same for an outsider as for a member, for the organization has more sanctions over members who, being more committed to it, cannot change organizations as easily.) However, even the independent entrepreneur is usually dependent upon organizations for his livelihood and must conform in some sense to gain their support and sanction.

The Oversocialized View of People

23   But let us focus on the individual who is a member of a large organization. Even he or she does not, and in fact probably cannot, commit fully to it. In the first place, the individual's allegiances will be split among the various organizations to which he or she belongs, such as civic clubs, churches, professional organizations, political parties, labor unions, and neighborhood groups. As a result, sometimes he or she will be trapped by conflicting pressures from different organizations. For example, the overtime demands on a factory worker might force cancellation of a place on the bowling team; or a labor union strike will force a choice between crossing the picket line or losing income and the good will of the management. But it is precisely these choices that give the individual some control over his or her life. The more inconsistency in the system, the more discretion that we as individuals will have in choosing among the different demands made on us; one set of norms can be used as a defense against others. At the same time, inconsistency provides the organization with ready alternatives when it must adapt to new circumstances: it can simply change emphasis. The net effect is that the "oversocialized" view of people, which portrays modern man and woman as mere conformists, ignores the variety of standards to which individuals choose to conform.

Deviance as Conformity

24   We are beginning to touch on the complexities of life in organizations. Each of us is trapped by a variety of stresses and competing strains that are inherent in the structure of many organizations. We often find ourselves in situations in which conforming to one expectation will automatically violate another. Sometimes the norms thmselves are incon-

16

sistent, and sometimes there is disagreement or ambiguity among the members about what the norms are. Often, the person is simultaneously involved in multiple roles as an employee, citizen, parent, and the like, with no clear blueprint for what action to take in a particular situation. Finally, we are all confronted with an overload because too much time or energy or skill is being demanded of us. Given these role conflicts, we cannot always "conform" to every norm, and on the surface it may seem that a person is being "deviant" or "obstinate." On closer inspection, however, we find that the person is probably conforming to some alternate norm.

Teachers are professional employees and are often confronted with conflicting choices between their professional and their employee roles. Their status as employees, where influence is based on position, is part of a strong tradition based on local control over educators. It is reinforced in the more recent growth of complex school systems that employ a high degree of administrative control for the sake of coordination. At the same time, aspiration to achieve professional status, where influence is based on technical expertise, points teachers in quite another direction. Professionals want to gain more control over their work (Corwin, 1967). For decades, teachers have subscribed to the idea that they have professional obligations, such as professional preparation and reading on their own time, and now many teachers also want professional rights, such as the right to select their own teaching strategy and materials. Membership in a teacher organization to promote or protect professionalism and rewards creates another conflict for teachers, sometimes forcing choices among what a teacher does as an individual, as an employee of a school district, and as a member of a teacher organization. [25]

What, then, is to be the fate of a teacher who is guilty of "insubordination" for attempting to protect students from a textbook or curriculum guide that he or she believes would be ineffective or even detrimental to the students? How will an otherwise competent teacher who leaves the building early be treated? The answers to these questions decide careers (Corwin, 1965). [26]

In this connection, one study compared school employees, police officers, and welfare workers on the degree to which each group stressed its professional and its employee roles (Peabody, 1964). The elementary school teachers attached more importance to the professional basis of their authority than the other two groups did. Yet the teachers' typical reaction to conflict was to acquiesce to the demands of their employee roles. That reaction was particularly characteristic of the less experienced members in the sample. [27]

WHAT IS THIS THING CALLED ORGANIZATION?

We have been talking blithely about organizations as though we all know what they are. We probably do in general terms. But it would help to agree on a precise definition so that we are clear about where our discussion applies and where it does not. There are many gray areas. For instance, how does an organization differ from a group? Are neighborhood play groups or work groups organizations? Is a family an organization? Is a bureaucracy an organization? [28]

A Simple Definition

Let us begin with this simple definition: An organization is a relatively permanent and complex social system (Haas and Drabeck, 1973). A formal organization is one that has been deliberately established (Blau, 1968). We will be concerned here primarily with formal organizations. Now, consider an example. [29]

30 **ODE TO THE PLAYGROUND COMMITTEE.** Suppose for a moment that some neighbors meet at a party and the discussion turns to the lack of local recreation facilities. The next day a neighbor calls you to a meeting to consider the prospect of establishing a playground, and you are delegated to find out how to do it. You ask for a committee to help; and the committee eventually drafts a proposal, submits it to the city council, and even lobbies some of the council members. The council refers the proposal to the city park commission which in turn requests assistance from the school system. The school system appoints several members from your group to one of its own committees concerned with such matters. In the meantime, an internal squabble develops and most of the original members of the neighborhood group resign. But you and a few members persevere, recruit new members, assess dues, and initiate a fund-raising drive. Officers are elected who in turn appoint four subcommittees (one of which begins to look into the possibility of establishing a new swimming pool). The new members of the committee, however, object that they are not being adequately represented.

31 The story goes on, of course, but we are less interested in the outcome than in the process. Is the playground committee an organization? If so, when did it become one? There is no precise moment. The organization evolved, and so its status at any one moment is a matter of degree. But we can agree that it became an organization when it was able to exist even after particular members left and when a division of labor had evolved. In this case, the decision to reappoint new members after the resignations, and the establishment of sub-committees, were crucial turning points.

A More Detailed Definition

32 But there are many features about the committee that are not explicitly reflected in this simple definition: conflict, authority relations, a sequence of activity, and the like. It might be useful then to include these features in our definition because they are shared in some degree by all complex, formal organizations. Here is a refinement and extension of the simple definition we started with: *An organization is a relatively permanent and complex social system that (a) consists of subgroups (or coalitions) and that has (b) a name and a location (that is, an unequivocal collective identity), (c) an exact roster of members, (d) an authority structure, (e) a division of labor, (f) a program of activity, and (g) procedures for replacing members* (Caplow, 1964; Corwin, 1967). As mentioned, this last criterion in itself makes a good simple test of the degree to which a group is organized. Also note that organizations consist of coalitions among groups, a fact that is important for understanding informal organizations, that is work groups, and the processes of conflict and change inherent in organizations.

33 Isn't something still missing? We have not said anything yet about the **purposes** of organizations. To some people, the purposefulness of organizations is the key to understanding them. These people define organizations as human groupings deliberately constructed and modified to seek specific goals (cf. Etzioni, 1964). Why have we not placed more stress on goals?

34 We agree that historically, most organizations were originally established for a certain purpose; and often this purpose remains clear many years later. However, purposes often change, or the organization's members and the people it serves simply lose sight of the purposes, or survival and/or growth supersede all other professed goals (Corwin, 1973). Often, the stated goals are merely rhetoric and have little effect on how the organization functions. Moreover, the goals are often a matter of perspective. For the customers, the goal of General Motors is to produce cars; for the workers, it is to provide jobs and income; for the stockholders, it is to make a profit; for the managers, it is perhaps to expand. The engineers and salespeople differ among themselves on the emphasis to be placed on secondary goals such as styling, speed, safety, fuel consumption, pollution, and the like. So the truth is, it is often much harder to ascertain the goals than the structure of an organization. Ultimately, clear goals may not be an essential characteristic of organizations! So it makes some sense to define organizations independently of their goals and then consider the extent to which a given organization has goals that can be identified through its tasks, reward system, and other activities.

Organizations Compared to Other Social Systems

So far we have focused on formal organizations. It might help us to understand organizations a little better by viewing them in a larger context, that is, by comparing them with other social systems. A *social system* can be defined as a set of lawfully related, highly stable, but complex relationships (Herriott and Hodgkins, 1973). An organization is a social system, but there are several types of social systems in addition to organizations. 35

It should be recognized that all social systems use and process materials, personnel, information, and other inputs which are discharged as manufactured products, services, graduates, and the like. Systems depend on communication back from the environment, tend to evolve into complex structural forms, and use various procedures to ensure stability in the face of a persistent tendency toward disintegration. 36

Social systems differ from one another in three important respects: their degree of permanence, their complexity, and the deliberateness with which they were established. For the sake of simplicity, let us first consider only the dimensions of complexity and permanence. A social gathering, such as a cocktail party or a beer group, is both a relatively simple and transitory or shortlived, social system. A gathering can evolve into a group, however, if the people meet together repeatedly, that is, if the gathering persists. Both gatherings and groups are relatively simple, differing in their degree of permanence. 37

Now consider other combinations of permanence and complexity. Societies and social movements, for example, are both quite complex but they differ in their permanence. Social movements are much more transitory than societies. In comparison, communities and social organizations range somewhere between these extremes, that is, they are relatively permanent and relatively complex (Haas and Drabeck, 1973). 38

Somebody Wanted It

Now we can add another consideration: the deliberateness with which the social system was established. Some groups, such as extended families, have evolved or emerged over time with very little deliberate planning or formal rules except for a legal (although vague) marriage contract. Many friendship groups, bridge clubs, and street gangs have evolved in much the same way. By contrast to these "emergent groups," others have been deliberately established, such as a neighborhood club requiring dues and officers. 39

Social systems, then, are characterized by their degree of permanence, their complexity, and the deliberateness with which they were established. A formal organization is one type of social system. 40

WHAT, THEN, IS A BUREAUCRACY?

41 Since most people are familiar with the term **bureaucracy,** it is important to consider it here. Although the term **bureaucracy** is sometimes used in a pejorative sense, it refers to a particular **type** of organization. Bureaucracies are organizations, but not all organizations are bureaucracies. Bureaucracy is a method of organizing administration in which experts rule under law. It consists of special jurisdictions of activity that are governed by rules and regulations, a system of graded levels of authority based on strict compliance of subordinates to the directions of their superiors, appointment to office on the basis of expert competence for a lifetime tenure, and a separation between the bureaucrat's personal life and his or her official vocation (Gerth and Mills, 1946).

42 Some sociologists believe that bureaucracy represents the ultimate form of rational efficiency. But many people see it as inefficient, cumbersome, unresponsive to change, and stifling to creativity. They argue that bureaucracies often concentrate power in the hands of a few self-appointed, often despotic, leaders.

43 Several critics have depicted the public schools as creaking bureaucracies in the most pejorative sense. In the satiric best seller, **Up the Down Staircase,** Kaufman (1966) sympathetically portrayed the anguish of teacher Sylvia Barret as she valiantly struggles through the bureaucratic hurdles of the New York City school system in a vain effort to reach a few of her students. She is overcome by her inept colleagues—the "desk despots," "blackboard barons," "classroom Caesars," and "lords of the looseleaf"—and is overwhelmed by seating plans, attendance sheets, requisitions, and the library blacklist. Depicted is a world of time clocks and mandatory meetings called for superficial discussions of democracy amidst a sea of tyranny. It is all run by the J.J. McHabes and Sadie Finches—the administrators and clerks—who, at every opportunity, spew out new memos bearing old directives: "Teachers who line up in front of the time clocks waiting to punch out in the afternoon create a crowded condition in the doorway" (p. 208) and "No written passes are to be issued to lavatories, since they are easily duplicated by the students. Only wooden lavatory passes are to be honored" (p. 12).

44 **110 Livingston Street** (Rogers, 1968) is another trenchant criticism of the inept backwardness of the New York City school administration and its paralysis in the face of serious issues confronting large-city schools. Despite a long list of policy statements adopted by the school board endorsing various plans to desegregate the New York City schools, action is blocked by a number of paralyzing bureaucratic pathologies. The school board is crippled by vested interests within the system and in the community, an inbred professional staff, and overcentralization. Decisions are made by people far removed from classrooms. Power is diffused, and responsibility is fragmented. The system is insulated from clientele, run by self-centered groups, isolated from city government.

Beyond Bureaucracy

45 However, these criticisms are oversimplified in several ways. First, even in the worst situations there is not one, but many **types** of organizations. Some authors believe that there is a trend away from bureaucracy to more complex types of organizations (Bennis and Slater, 1968). Irrespective of whether there is a trend, there is already much variability. Havighurst (1964) identified four types of elementary schools located within Chicago's city limits, each with enormous differences in pupil achievement, family backgrounds of children, teacher attitudes, and teaching styles. Organizations do not seem to become highly bureaucratic except in the most troublesome and chaotic conditions.

46 Second, even highly bureaucratic organizations are not necessarily created by incompetent, malicious, and calloused people with so-called "bureaucratic personalities."

Teachers have been portrayed as mindless employees blindly enforcing the rules, loyal to inept administrators, and so overspecialized that they cannot see students as human beings, preferring instead to spend their time on trivia such as collecting lunch money, taking attendance, and keeping up with the daily lesson plan. But the fundamental problems usually stem from structural weaknesses, not alone from the tyranny or incompetence of the people involved. Even if there were no tyrants or incompetents in teaching, many of the problems would persist.

Third, some problems arise when organizations are not bureaucratic enough. For example, although one of the criticisms of schools is that they are overcentralized, in fact, the superintendent of schools in New York City lacks even the most essential power of a strong executive—the power to appoint or remove key assistants who are protected by tenure. [47]

Finally, even many traditional, "old line" bureaucracies are undergoing significant transformations. Through systems of "participatory democracy," for example, even low-ranking employees can have some voice in decisions that affect them. Similarly, simple authority hierarchies do not reflect the influence that labor unions and professional associations have on management decisions. The growing influence of specialists is another complication. Purchasing officers, budget analysts, architects, engineers, lawyers, researchers, management and personnel consultants, logistics experts, and other specialists typically do not have "line" authority over most of the employees, but through their advice to top management, they shape policy more than their formal position suggests. Military rank, for example, has been literally transformed because of the influence of specialists on the decisions of command officers. And then, too, the formerly simple act of delegation has become quite complicated by the growing reliance on subcontracts through which one organization pays another to perform some of its tasks. For example, school districts may contract for food service, police protection, or even the teaching of certain subjects. Administrators have very different types of relationships with the teachers employed on a subcontract than with their own employees. [48]

Of course, these changes apply to some organizations more than to others, but there are enough complications to suggest that one should be cautious about applying the label "bureaucracy" to modern organizations. [49]

IS THERE A RELIABLE "THEORY" OF ORGANIZATIONS?

The term *theory* may seem a little presumptuous because, as we have just seen, knowledge in this field is at best fragmentary. But it is a little like the question, "How is your husband or your wife?" Compared to what? None of the behavioral science theories (including those in psychology and economics) matches the sophistication and predictive power of many theories developed in the physical sciences, but that does not mean that social science has made no progress over conventional wisdom. [50]

Theory: Something for Everyone

Theory means many different things (Merton, 1957(a)). It often implies *codified knowledge.* For example, there are known and systematic relationships in the size of an organization, the level at which decisions are made, and patterns of supervision (Blau, 1970). These relationships have been codified as theorems, major propositions, corollaries, and the like. This kind of codified knowledge is rather rare, however. More typically, theory in this field refers to the testing of isolated hypotheses or ad hoc interpretations of events that have already occurred. [51]

21

52   One of the most controversial uses of the term *theory* concerns the development and application of concepts. To the lay person, this often seems like substituting jargon for common language. However, as the term theory itself illustrates, commonly used terms are not clear because they are packed with diverse meanings and values. A new concept can bring to conscious awareness knowledge that might have only been implicit before.

53   The term *theory* is used here to refer to general orientations or approaches, a set of assumptions about how an organization operates, some of which have been tested, some of which have not. There has been a dispute over general approaches to the study of organizations. People who study them seem to have two fundamentally different models in mind, each of which leads to very different advice (Gouldner, 1959).

Will the "Real" Organization Theorist Please Stand Up?

54   The diversity of points of view about organizations provides richness in perspective but also creates considerable confusion. Psychologists approach the topic by trying to understand how individuals learn to cope with organizations. Social psychologists approach it from the view of small work groups within larger organizations. Sociologists are concerned with larger units and have attempted to isolate organizations—for example, to determine how business corporations differ from those in human services or how large and small organizations differ from one another. For the sociologist, a single organization is only one in a large population of organizations operating on distinctive principles based on structural, not individual, relationships.

Are Organizations Real?

55   Like the blind men with the elephant, each theorist finds a different reality because he or she starts with different kinds of questions or problems. Psychologists ask about the psychological attributes of individuals, such as their attitudes toward people in authority. Social psychologists want to know how a person's behavior is affected by membership in groups or organizations. For example, is one more likely to quit one's job if one has few friendships at work? Does one's work history depend on age, sex, marital status, and the like? Sociologists work with several different kinds of variables, including (a) distributions of individuals, such as the proportion of men to women; (b) stable relationships between people in different positions, such as the average frequency of contact between teachers and principals; and (c) the integral attributes of organizations, such as the number of departments or the number of authority levels (Lazarsfeld and Menzel, 1969). Most of these characteristics cannot be derived from information about individuals, and even information based on individuals says more about the organization than about an individual or group.

56   It can be seen from these last illustrations that organizations consist of more than people. Understanding people helps, of course, but it is not enough. This is not to deny the importance of individuals. Rather, it is to recognize that many important features of organizations derive from their structures and functions—hierarchies, divisions of labor, decision-making systems, and so on. To the extent that individuals are considered, the focus must be on individuals viewed collectively. Because most of us have been conditioned to think of organizations primarily as collections of individuals, we often assume that we can understand organizations on the basis of our personal experiences. But personal experiences are simply not sufficient; there are emergent qualities that transcend the individuals involved. Only by subjecting a large sample of organizations to sophisticated methods of analysis can we observe, for example, what happens to the level at

which decisions are made or to the ratio of employees to supervisors as organizations become larger.

HOW DO THEORISTS APPROACH
THE STUDY OF ORGANIZATIONS?

There are at least four different general orientations to organizations based on different persuasions in psychology, social psychology, sociology, and other behavioral sciences. Each discipline approaches the subject from its own frame of reference, its own traditions, and its own motivations or reasons. [57]

The *management approach* emphasizes the study of organizations as a means to develop a body of techniques for impersonally controlling workers from the top, especially by manipulating aspects of the structure such as rules, procedures, and the optimum ratio of supervisors to employees. Because productivity is a major goal, importance is attached to time-and-motion studies and the science of aptitude testing. This approach is best suited to organizations characterized by uniform and recurrent (that is, unambiguous) events that can be handled through rules or standard techniques. The argument is that any other approach would be less efficient. Because of the emphasis on impersonal control, advocates of this approach show little regard for the values and desires of the workers. Accordingly, this has been referred to as the "organizations without people" approach (Peabody, 1964). [58]

By contrast, the *human relations approach* might be called the "people without organizations" approach. The personal elements of work groups and the job satisfaction and morale of workers are central concerns. This approach is best suited to human-service organizations and those in which events are not uniform and there are many unique problems. Stress is placed on social skills, such as the ability to communicate with and influence individuals or small groups. The theory is that it would not be effective to use any other approach. But again, productivity is often an ulterior objective; a happy worker is assumed to be an efficient worker, and participating in decisions is assumed to increase commitment to the organization. The approach also leans heavily on changing the employees through training, although the sources of problems often lie in the market situation, history, tradition, the incentive system, the size and complexity of the organization, its technology, and other such factors. This larger picture can easily become obscured by a preoccupation with human relations. [59]

Both approaches were designed to increase productivity and efficiency and, to a lesser extent in the case of human relations in service organizations, to "humanize" aspects of the organizations. Advocates of these approaches are preoccupied with variables that can be manipulated by management. Neither approach was designed primarily for the purpose of understanding or explaining organizations. The organization is used only as a setting for improving supervision of work groups. [60]

The *personality-organization approach* is a variant of these two. Emphasis is placed on the conflict between (a) the personality needs of individuals for independence, variety, and challenge; and (b) the preference that organizations give to placid, dependent, and submissive employees (Argyris, 1957). Again, the focus is on how individuals cope with organizations rather than on organizations per se; organizations are treated primarily as a setting for the study of personality problems. [61]

Sociological approaches are concerned with structural characteristics inherent in organizations—for example, their size, complexity, number of levels of authority, degree [62]

23

of specialization, formalization, standardization, functional autonomy, and technology. These characteristics establish boundaries within which people must live, conditions of life, and options available.

63 Max Weber, an early observer of bureaucracies, was concerned with what the rationalization of modern organizations would do to the value of individualism (Henderson and Parsons, 1947). This approach has been criticized for being dehumanizing and fatalistic because it ignores the feelings of individual members and presumes that behavior is predetermined by social norms. Actually Weber's work highlighted what happens to individuals within organizations.

64 A compromise was proposed by Litwak (1961). In his view, most organizations deal with both uniform and nonuniform situations and therefore develop characteristics of both the human-relations and structural approaches. Litwak calls this the "professional" model. In this model, the different procedures used are segregated through various mechanisms including separation of roles, physical distance, differences among occupational groups in the organization, and evaluation procedures.

WHERE DOES THE INDIVIDUAL STAND IN ALL THIS?

65 To answer that question adequately would take at least as many additional pages as you have already read. But in summary, most individuals are in the middle of a complex, interdependent collection of organizations. Most of us have primary affiliation with and membership in just a few. We have considerable choice, on the one hand, in deciding which organizations we will belong to but we exercise that choice at some cost, either in the risks of becoming independent enough to select and move among organizations, or in the price we must pay in conformity if we choose to belong to a more limited selection of organizations—for example, those that are more easily accessible by virtue of our training, experience, ability, locale, and social class. However, within the organizations that most of us join, there is considerable latitude for movement without being completely coopted; there is the possibility of exerting influence for change and improvement, and there is the possibility of gaining the wisdom to know what can be changed and the wisdom to live with what is inevitable.

66 There is also the possibility of developing commitment to the basic goals of an organization—becoming part of an organization and having it become part of you (sometimes a very satisfying intermesh of individual and organization). There is also the possibility of overcommitment—reaching a point where self-goals and organization goals become indistinguishable—a situation not to be recommended if personal identity is an important value. The goal of many thoughful people who prize individuality and personal dignity is to find a middle ground between extremes of personal commitment to and identification with an organization. They take care to relate to more than the organization, so that life has variety and richness and so that several options are open in the event of crisis or impossible situational developments.

67 The major point is that being aware of and understanding the phenomena of organizations provides a kind of insurance that choices can be more rational, and that intelligence and personal preference can be employed in coping with or attempting to influence change in the organizations in which we live.

Section 2: What Are Organizations Like?

Ronald G. Corwin   Roy A. Edelfelt

HOW ARE ORGANIZATIONS ORGANIZED?

We have said that to cope effectively with organizations, a person must first understand them. Social scientists do not fully understand organizations, but more is known than we can deal with here. Let us confine our attention to some of their *key* features. Organizations are obviously "organized," but the question is: How?   68

Key Features of Organizations

We shall begin with some fundamental characteristics of organizations and then refine and build on them as the chapter progresses. We will not presume to be inclusive here, but the concepts discussed below are important and will help to illustrate the kinds of information that one would need to begin an analysis of an organization.   69

In thinking about organization, it is often helpful to distinguish between (a) the formal characteristics which are an integral part of the organization's structure, such as the number of departments, levels in the hierarchy, size, etc; and (b) its operational characteristics, such as the prestige system, friendship cliques, and the like. It is also possible to visualize both the structural and operational aspects of organizations along two other dimensions: a vertical, or hierarchical, dimension and a horizontal dimension, which applies to peers. After describing how organizations are divided up on the vertical and horizontal dimensions, we shall discuss some of the ways they are reintegrated.   70

Up (and Down) the Organization

The vertical dimension of structure can be seen in the official rank of people holding different positions of authority. However, as the organization actually operates, people may have more or less prestige, influence, responsibility, or income than their formal rank warrants. That is, as members of an organization, all are ranked on one and often several different hierarchies based on power, authority, responsibility, prestige, esteem, competence, income, and the like.   71

Therefore, each of these dimensions must be considered if one is fully to understand an organization. **Power** refers to the ability of one party to impose its will on another, even if the effort is resisted. When there is a high probability that power can be applied, it is often referred to as control; when the probability is lower, it is called influence. Power increases with the number of sanctions available to the person exercising it, and it diminishes as those sanctions are actually applied. That is, an employer has more power when threatening to fire an employee than after the employee has been fired. People often have more, or less, power than they are authorized to use.   72

Authority refers to the legitimate right to exercise power. However, there are several sources of authority, and they do not always agree. This places authority in jeopardy. For example, legally an employer may be required to prohibit smoking among employees on the job, but the employees may dispute that right. Teacher strikes are seldom authorized by law, but they are usually supported by the majority of members and by many citizens.   73

25

74   *Responsibility* refers to work obligations assigned to people, groups, or organizations. Sometimes people involved do not have the necessary power or technical ability to carry out their responsibilities. Teachers, for example, are held accountable for teaching good citizenship, reducing delinquency, and motivating pupils, in addition to teaching subject matter. The necessary technical skills are better developed for some of these tasks than for others. Similarly, many school boards believe that it is unfair for the courts to hold them responsible for desegregating the schools since segregation is also tied to housing patterns and public opinion about busing.

75   *Prestige* refers to the way a position is appraised and valued by general opinion. Individuals can claim prestige, but it derives from the position they hold. For example, teachers of English literature in comprehensive high schools generally have more prestige than teachers of vocational subjects even though the latter might have more influence on certain aspects of school policy.

76   *Esteem* is the way an individual's performance is appraised and valued. Teachers have more prestige than janitors, but a particular janitor may be held in higher esteem than many teachers. Esteem is often based on the person's technical competence, but it is not confined to that. It may be based on the individual's values or experience.

77   *Competence* refers to an objective measure of the ability of an individual or group to perform responsibilities. It may be related to a group's training or experience, but competence is also determined by how far the technology of an occupation has advanced. An entire occupation may be judged incompetent to carry out certain responsibilities it is trying to achieve.

78   *Status inconsistency* describes the fact that we may find ourselves in different places on different hierarchies, and we can easily become trapped in inconsistent expectations. For example, we may have high prestige in the organization, but make less money than people with lower prestige, or the opposite. How much deference, then, are we supposed to show other people and they us?

79   This kind of inconsistency can have important effects on an organization. For example, inconsistencies between the power and authority of employees, compared to the restraints on them, seem to promote militant collective actions among employees (Corwin, 1975). There is some evidence that when teachers have opportunities to participate in decisions in school systems, they tend to become militant (Corwin, 1970; 1975). If they are already participating in decisions, why do they rebel? One reason may be that there are more rules and regulations in decentralized than in centralized systems. Their authority is restrained by bureaucratic procedures. Similarly, their actual collective power often is not acknowledged in the amount of authority, that is, the right to exercise power, that they are granted by the school board; so they use collective actions to demonstrate their power.

80   Consider some examples of discrepancies in power and authority in familiar positions in a public school system. A school principal is technically and often legally responsible for many events and activities in the school, even though he or she may not know that they are taking place or could not control them in any event. Power is usually diffused throughout organizational hierarchies. Principals do not have control over many events that affect teachers every day, such as the fact that the central warehouse was supposed to deliver the books over three weeks ago. For example, it is difficult for a principal to be familiar with all of the supplementary reading materials that teachers in the school might be assigning to students. And even if the principal were familiar with them and a group of parents objected to a particular book, he or she might try to censor the book only at the

risk of a confrontation with the teachers' union, determined to protect the teachers' authority over such matters. Yet, as members of an organization, we are often inclined to blindly hold administrative superiors accountable, without considering discrepancies between their apparent authority and their actual power.

Similarly, administrators often hold their subordinates responsible for events that [81] they cannot control very well. Teachers frequently complain that it is unfair to hold them responsible for the performance of students who do not want to be in school in the first place. (One proposal that teachers have made to alleviate this particular problem is to abandon legal compulsory attendance.) Given these discrepancies among power, authority, and responsibility, it is not always entirely clear who has the actual power to resolve a problem when it arises.

Emulation refers to the ways in which subordinates copy superiors. Most people at [82] some time find themselves in the middle of a hierarchy where they must cope with inconsistent expectations from people above and those below. The classroom teacher is such a person in the middle—between the principal who expects the teacher to promote academic achievement and maintain discipline, and students who prefer to make their own choices and to have freedom of movement. One of the intriguing things about hierarchies is the way people at the top of the hierarchy act toward subordinates often is reflected in the actions of people in the lower echelons. For example, if a factory foreman is being pushed by his supervisor for more production or if he is being watched closely, then he is likely to behave in the same way toward the men and women whom he is supervising. You might notice how these pressures affect your own behavior when you move from one organization to another. For example, suppose you are a teacher who is used to being open and relaxed with your students and you then transfer to a school where the principal "runs a tight ship." You may very well find yourself becoming more strict about classroom discipline than you prefer or even than you realize. Or compare your response to a college fraternal organization you belong to in which the rules are informal and permissive, with your behavior in a formal college classroom or in church.

This tendency for subordinates to copy the supervisory style of their supervisors is [83] so pervasive that subordinates often go to greater extremes than superiors really expect.

Delegation is handing of responsibility to subordinates by people at the top. Prob- [84] lems may arise in this process. Often, superiors do not delegate the power and authority necessary to carry out the responsibilities. For example, a school nurse is delegated the responsibility for providing health services to students in a school but does not have the authority to administer some drugs, perhaps even aspirin, in treating minor maladies. In addition, subordinates frequently find that they must carry out policies they did not formulate and often do not understand or support. Policies are formulated in general terms and must be reinterpreted at each level of the hierarchy in order to apply the policies to the concrete realities. This leaves a lot of latitude for personal views, including fears, to shape the way one interprets and applies the general policy.

Slippage describes the changes that occur as policy is passed down the hierarchy. [85] There is a great deal of slippage between the intent of a policy as formulated at the top of a hierarchy and the way it is finally carried out by subordinates (Corwin, 1974). This slippage also occurs in the other direction, from the bottom to the top. That is, the information communicated to supervisors becomes distorted at each level as it is reinterpreted and filtered. For example, a teacher who cannot maintain discipline in the classroom might be reluctant to admit this fact to his or her supervisor. The amount of slippage increases with the number of levels in the hierarchy. Contrary to some popular stereotypes, employees often have more latitude in big organizations than in small ones because there is more slippage (Blau, 1970; Corwin, 1975 (b)).

86 This same type of slippage, by the way, is inherent in the long chain of decision points between the federal government and local school boards. Although it is conceivable that federal agencies might influence local schools, that influence is seldom as great as either conservatives fear or liberals hope—because of the slippage factor.

Across the Organization

87 In addition to these vertical hierarchies, organizations have a horizontal dimension. This is reflected in the formal structure by the separate departments, programs, specialties, buildings, and so on. For example, this division of labor can be observed in high schools which are organized by grade levels, departments, programs, tracks, and the like. But, of course, people are not confined to a formal niche. Friendships, lines of communication, and patterns of assistance usually cut across formal divisions. And, within a given division, employees with the same job may be split by differences in experience, philosophy, sex, or disputes about their responsibilities.

88 *Zones of autonomy* are work assignments which the employee performs independently of others. Some jobs either require or permit more autonomy than others. These zones of autonomy create coordination problems, in that they provide a great deal of discretion to some employees. Specialists often compete with specialists in other areas. For example, rivalries often arise between teachers of academic subjects and those in athletics, or between teachers of the fundamentals and those in the more practical fields. In many communities, coaches connected with the athletic program manage to achieve a great deal of autonomy because the program is independently financed by public admissions or community booster clubs (Corwin, 1970). This autonomy helps to protect the athletic program from other teachers on the staff who may not think it is as important as some members of the community do.

89 When zones of autonomy are coupled with "structural looseness," employees have a wide degree of latitude, if they choose to use it. People in lower echelons often have much more power than is publicly acknowledged or even than they themselves fully recognize. In particular, any employee who must deal with nonroutine matters is in a position to influence the organization. And any employee can influence the work schedule through the amount of effort he or she is willing to expend; the employee can also screen out information and enter into coalitions of employees, such as associations or unions. With such factors in mind, Lortie (1969) concluded that school teachers have far more autonomy than generally is acknowledged and that, far from feeling frustrated by confining rules and regulations, teachers are often satisfied with their status in schools.

90 **WHAT DOES IT MEAN TO HAVE AUTONOMY?** However, we should be clear about what this autonomy actually means to employees. First, employees often do not take advantage of the discretion that is available to them. It is easier to follow routine than to exercise choice. Moreover, many employees are not fully aware of the range of choices available to them—which is a major reason why they can benefit if they have more knowledge about and skill in analyzing organizations. Second, we do not want to exaggerate the significance of autonomy. For us, autonomy is nothing more than the discretion that a person has to choose among already fixed alternatives. It is not the same as power, which is the ability to establish these alternatives. Teachers may be "permitted" to make some choices, but, by its nature, permission can be withdrawn. Nor is discretion

the same thing as being insulated or not closely watched. Often our feeling of freedom is heightened when we are not being closely observed, but this does not mean that we have more freedom of choice. Close supervision, after all, is only one way in which employees are controlled.

Power is the ability to produce results. Autonomy, in the sense of either discretion or insulation, is far less consequential than power, which tends to be centralized in school systems. How much power do teachers actually have to determine whether or not a course will be required, how subject matter will be sequenced, what textbooks will be used, which students will be admitted and promoted, how children will be disciplined, or even which methods will be used in the classroom? The little discretion that teachers have in these matters is relatively circumscribed and often trivial. They are constrained by curriculum guides, textbooks, standardized tests, and tradition. Lortie (1969) stated the relationship between power and autonomy succinctly: "Succeeding layers of administration narrow the range of goal selections possible at the teacher level, but persons at that level may be free to choose among the goals that remain" (pp. 12-13). It almost appears that at the lower levels of the hierarchy, the discretion available is inversely correlated with power; that is, employees purchase their autonomy by giving up their opportunities to influence the fundamental conditions of their work. Most of us could benefit by thinking about how much discretion is available, where the limits of this discretion lie, and how we might go about influencing these limits. This could lead to autonomy that is legitimized in the organization rather than permitted at the price of conformity.

Putting It All Together

Most of the characteristics we have mentioned have the effect of splintering organizations into separate parts: echelons, departments, cliques, etc. But we hasten to mention again that the features being described are actually variables—they differ from one organization to another. Therefore, coordination will pose a greater problem in some organizations than in others. But generally speaking, all organizations would disintegrate under the forces just described without some means of coordination. As employees, we are all expected to comply with some procedures, whether or not we personally agree with them, in order to maintain some consistency in the system as a whole. However, various organizations attempt to achieve coordination in different ways.

Standardization is a systematic set of procedures. It is one way to achieve coordination. Standardization can include uniform rules, curriculum guides, textbooks, and lesson plans for courses taught throughout the school system. Mass education would probably be impossible without some assurances of uniformity. Rules established as general policy have protected education from the patronage of corrupt city government and have protected teachers from the arbitrary decisions of administrators. Also, general policy rules are less personally threatening to individuals than, for example, each individual being told what to do by a supervisor.

But standardization also has unintended effects. First, in a pluralistic society such as ours, many people do not fit the standards. For example, curricula that seem adequate for some middle-class youngsters have been grossly ineffective for large numbers of low-income children, and yet teachers cannot readily adapt to different types of children when they are judged only on standard tests of student performance and a middle-class expectation of student behavior. As another example, labeling lower-class students as "drop-outs" or "underachievers" on the basis of intelligence tests places the blame on the students instead of on the organization.

95   As a general principle, service organizations that are established to deal with special problems seem to give preference to the clients who are most likely to be visibly helped and therefore are only marginally afflicted with those problems. They select clients for whom it is easy to demonstrate that measurable improvement has been accomplished in order to achieve their quotas. For example, agencies established to deal with the blind prefer to deal with individuals with partial sight, and physical rehabilitation agencies prefer people who have only one physical handicap rather than those who have many different kinds of handicaps.

96   Although not intended, rules usually establish only the minimal behavior that is required by the organization (Gouldner, 1954). It is difficult for organizations officially to require employees to exert extraordinary effort; and yet if all employees followed the literal rules, it is doubtful that the organization could function. One way to ruin an organization is for everyone to follow every rule to the letter and to do nothing more. So each rule seems to encourage more, not less, direct supervision.

97   Nor is it intended that rules be enforced selectively but they usually are. Rules can be seen as the poker chips in a personal bargaining situation. That is, supervisors use rules to bargain for the employee's loyalty. For example, they will be lenient toward tardiness, the no-smoking rules, or the use of first names only as long as the employees otherwise perform properly. They enforce the rules strictly with respect to individuals who are not committed to their goals. Rules also are often used to justify a decision that already has been made on other grounds. For example, if there are two employees and one goes out of the way to please the supervisor while the other does not, and if both employees are consistently late for work, the latter one is more likely to be reprimanded for being late too often.

98   Finally, rules inadvertently seem to block change and inhibit interaction of members with outsiders (Corwin, 1975 (a); Corwin and Wagenaar, 1975). It is often difficult to comply with rules when you are being pressured to do something new or to work closely with outsiders who do not have to live up to the rules. Potential conflicts of this sort can be averted by avoiding outsiders and persons who want to change the rules. As a result, however, the organization may be less responsive to its clientele. Also, when people do choose to take action against an organization, they often confine their grievances to "red tape," that is, rules enforced by low-echelon employees. Because complaints aimed at this level do not challenge the basic structure or policies of the organization, they divert attention from the fundamental problems. Hence, attacks on red tape ultimately have a conservative effect, according to Gouldner (1952).

99   *Direct supervision* is the overseeing of one employee by another. It allows for surveillance and two-way communication as ways of facilitating coordination. It can be productive provided there is mutual commitment to desired outcomes and that there are provisions to insure employees will be treated fairly.

100   *Mutual Adjustment* is a form of coordination based on informal communications or shared ideologies. For example, one teacher may learn over lunch that another teacher is planning a field trip the next week and so may postpone his or her own field trip, or perhaps they may arrange a joint field trip so they can share the same bus.

101   *Scheduling,* the organizing of employees work patterns into specific, required time frames, is still another alternative. For example, having all employees on the job at 8:30 a.m. coordinates all other activities. Consider the problems of coordination if each employee signed up for 20, 30, or 40 hours a week, scheduled any time between 8:30 a.m. and midnight.

Reporting, the systematic collection and compilation of various types of informa- 102
tion, also occurs very often. Most organizations gather and report data in a variety of
forms. Typical examples would include employee evaluations, time sheets, and periodic
audits. This list is probably endless to people in very large organizations. Often the forms
only indicate that something is happening but tell little about the quality of what is happening. Assessing the life success of a graduating class is all but impossible. Reporting how
many students graduated, how many went to college, how many went into the serivce,
etc. is relatively easy.

Sometimes different forms of coordination are not entirely consistent. Employees 103
may be trapped by conflicting rules, supervisory expectations, and their own value
systems. How individuals cope with such circumstances is discussed in paragraphs 138
through 145.

WHAT KINDS OF ORGANIZATIONS ARE THERE?

So far, we have been talking about features that all organizations share, but in vary- 104
ing degrees. But, there are different kinds of organizations and there may be vast differences within any one of them. As members of organizations, we all need to be aware of
these differences as we encounter them. The problem is that there is no completely satis-
factory way to classify them. But let us see what has been proposed.

Two Basic Models

There has been a dispute over general approaches to the study of organizations. 105
People who study them seem to have two fundamentally different models in mind, each
of which leads to very different advice (Gouldner, 1959). In the "rational model," persons in positions of authority also possess the necessary expertise. In the "organic
model," on the other hand, formal authority, as reflected in rank or title, is not necessarily indicative of expertise, and subordinates owe deference to the boss because of position regardless of that person's expertise.

There are some other differences which are important. The following assumptions 106
underlie the rational model:

- Organizations have clear-cut goals that are understood and subscribed to by
  members.
- Activities are well planned.
- Activities are closely coordinated.
- The necessary information is available for making the informed decisions
  necessary to achieve the goals.
- Control is centralized, and officials have sufficient control over the organization
  to ensure compliance with long-range plans.
- Formal authority (rank) is supported by a corresponding level of expertise.

In short, "rationality" results from a well integrated system produced by firm con- 107
trol from enlightened administrators. The structure appears to be entirely manipulable
and designed solely for purposes of efficiency. Significant changes are due to planned
efforts to increase efficiency, and any departures from rationality can be attributed to
rational mistakes, ignorance, or miscalculation. The keys to this model, then, are administrative control, expertise, and integration of the various components of the organization.

The following assumptions underlie the organic model:

108

- Members in different parts of an organization, math teachers, coaches, or janitors, often place the interests and objectives of their own unit above those prescribed for the overall organization.

- One's status and activities in an organization take on value as ends in themselves independent of demonstrated contributions to explicit goals.

- The official goals tend to change or are neglected as the organization strains to survive or expand; the survival needs take precedence over other goals.

- Decisions are the outcomes of bargaining and compromise among competing subgroups.

- No one group has sufficient information or power to compel a high degree of coordination among the subgroups.

- Formal authority (rank) is not necessarily derived from expertise; no two bases of authority are independent.

In the organic model, organization "policy" accumulates increasingly and in an unplanned manner. Members inadvertently commit the organization to certain "goals" in the process of bargaining with each other and with outsiders.

109
These two models—rational and organic—lead to very different conclusions about the relative importance of (a) consensus on goals and (b) power and conflict in organizations. If consensus is assumed to be the primary feature, then organizations will be seen as stable and harmonious and employees will be willing to comply with requests, or at least they can be persuaded to do so. If power is assumed to be the primary feature, then organizations will be characterized by change, conflict, and disintegration, and employees will obey only if coerced; they can be expected to rebel against the hierarchy when the opportunity arises (Dahrendorf, 1959).

110
As mentioned, the models also seem to lead to different types of advice about how to solve problems. Following the rational model, one would expect that problems can be solved by stressing clarification of goals, better long-range planning, more effective communication, and better information. But the organic model seems to point to quite different types of strategies: reorganization, alteration of the power structure, more frequent bargaining, and the use of conflict regulating devices like arbitration.

On the Other Hand

111
A middle ground is represented by writers who see organizations as tension-management systems. Conflict is present but is constrained by agreement on the basic objectives and by norms about propriety. Differences of opinion and interest are resolved through collective bargaining and individual negotiation. Organizations are then portrayed as systems of "negotiated order" (cf. Corwin, 1973, pp. 350-53).

112
Probably each of these views is more applicable to some organizations than others. That is, value consensus, conflict, or negotiation may be more prevalent in some organizations than in others. Even the same organization will vary from one time to the next.

113
The structure of the organization has something to do with this variation (Coser, 1956). If the organization has a relatively loose structure, conflict can erupt easily, but because personal allegiance shifts from one conflict to another, major divisions do not form. Conflict is a tension-management mechanism in such structures. But in a rigidly structured organization, there are fewer outlets for the expression of disagreements and when conflict breaks out, major divisions form among the groups involved.

These two basic models help to expose the main differences in underlying assump-   114
tions that we can make about organizations. Organizations quite possibly differ among
themselves in the degree to which they conform to each model. Further, some parts of a
given organization may be more like the rational model, while others function more like
the organic model. These differences also might change over time or with changes in the
environment. There may be some effective compromise between the two models. So, the
models can be useful for comparing several schools in a given city; departments, grade
levels, or echelons within a school; or for describing historical changes.

Typologies

But for some purposes, it may be useful to focus on only one or two features of   115
these models when comparing organizations. The main differences between two organizations might lie in their goals, in their systems of coordination, in their authority structure,
or in their products. So, let us consider some of these more specific classification systems,
i.e., "typologies."

WHO BENEFITS? One way of classifying organizations is based on their goals, or the   116
primary beneficiary of the organization's activities (Blau and Scott, 1962): (a) in *mutual
benefit* associations—for example labor unions or teacher organizations—the rank-and-file
participants are the primary beneficiaries; (b) in *business* concerns, beneficiaries are the
owners or managers; (c) in *service* organizations, such as schools and hospitals, they are
the clients; and (d) in *commonweal* organizations, such as police departments, the public
at large benefits. Each type of organization poses unique problems for its members. For
example, employees encounter the most conflict between professional and administrative
norms in service organizations where organizational principles often impair the professional's ability to render service to clients.

MEANS OF CONTROL. Another typology has two dimensions (Etzioni, 1961):   117

1. The kinds of sanctions the organization employs—coercive (force), remunerative
   (giving members money to participate), or normative (moral chastisement); and
2. The degree of membership involvement—alienative (negative toward the organization), calculative (a neutral, contractual relationship), and moral (positive commitment to the values and activities of the organization).

The "congruent" cells of these two dimensions produce three types of organizations: 118

1. Order-type (coercive) organizations, which consist of an alienated membership and
   which use coercive forms of control, as exemplified by prisons or forced labor
   camps;
2. Economic-type (utiltarian) organizations, which rely on money to secure the efforts
   of essentially neutral members, as exemplified by factories; and
3. Culture-type (normative) organizations, the members of which are morally involved
   with the norms and committed to the goals, as exemplified by universities, schools,
   clubs, fraternities, general hospitals, political organizations, labor unions, voluntary
   associations, and so forth.

In several respects schools are more similar to other coercive organizations than they   119
are to churches or moral organizations. For example, even if we acknowledge wide variations in the nature of both schools and prisons, there are some apparent similarities:

33

- *Recruitment:* Attendance is compulsory for both students and prisoners, and the organizations have few options in selecting their membership.
- *Goals:* The custodial goals (namely, to keep members off the streets) frequently take precedence over the therapeutic, educational, or socialization goals.
- *Supervision:* Control is extended over the total life of both students and inmates, including restrictions on their freedom to move about the building, to obtain a drink of water, to use restrooms, to dress as they wish; misbehavior is entered in official records; punishment is not administered through the local system; and the individual is not represented by a third party.
- *Authority:* There is little opportunity for either students or inmates to influence major policy decisions.
- *Power:* Both inmates and students are discouraged from organizing collectively for activities other than those sponsored by the organization; and their leaders often are coopted by the administration as a condition for obtaining official recognition and support for their group activities (such as the newspaper).
- *Rules:* Life in both prisons and schools is highly routinized, with schedules standardized for individuals and/or classes of individuals.
- *Careers:* Promotions are contingent on having served a specified length of time, good behavior, and evidence of having achieved minimal skills necessary to obtain work upon leaving the organization.
- *Boundary maintenance:* Relatives or other interested third parties cannot obtain entree into the organization without permission and then only for specifically stated purposes or events.

120   **HOW DID THE MEMBERS GET THERE?** Still another typology is based on the way members are recruited: (a) whether the organization can select its own members; and (b) whether the members can refuse to participate. These two dimensions together form four types of organizations (Carlson, 1964). In type I, the organization selects members, either by formal or informal means, and they participate on a voluntary basis. Private universities, hospitals, and doctors' offices are good examples. Many of the public-welfare service units apply stringent criteria in the selection of clients, and the potential client cannot be compelled to accept the service. The second type of organization, type II, does not select its members, and participation is not mandatory. This type is illustrated by those state universities legally required to accept all high school graduates who wish to enroll. Type III, which is relatively rare, selects its members and they are compelled to participate. This is characteristic of a citizen army based on a draft. Finally, in type IV, neither the organization nor its members have much choice. There are a number of organizations of this type including public schools, state mental hospitals, reform schools, and prisons. By law or tradition, clients of these organizations are required to participate, and the organizations have little choice about which clients they will serve. Such organizations usually have been guaranteed survival: they seldom have to compete for members, and their funds are not usually tied to the quality of performance because the processes of teaching and learning are complex, intangible, and difficult to assess.

121   The type of organization would make a difference to the members. For example, you would probably be least motivated to participate in types III and IV because you and other members did not necessarily choose to be there. This lack of motivation, in turn, would influence the attitudes of staff and members toward each other, their personality make-up, prestige of the work, and the way in which resources are used. Bureaucratic regulations are likely to be a major problem in types II and IV. Because such organizations do not control admission, they probably will not rely on the voluntary compli-

ance of members (who may not share objectives). One response is to segregate the less motivated members in "dumping grounds" (as illustrated by some vocational programs in high schools).

TECHNIQUE. Organizations also can be classified according to the reliability of the technology used and the diversity of the raw materials and problems dealt with (Perrow, 1970). For example, a craft is an industry that relies on rather uncertain techniques to handle routine problems. Engineering firms, on the other hand, apply reliable techniques to a variety of problems. The typology can be applied to both product manufacturing firms and *people-changing* (service) organizations.   122

In people-changing organizations, "reliability of the technology" means the degree to which the problems of clients are understood and therefore can be dealt with. Using this approach, we can identify four types of people-changing organizations: 123

1. Those with uniform clientele whose problems are not well understood (for example, ghetto schools)
2. Those with uniform clientele whose problems are well understood (for example, custodial institutions, vocational training)
3. Those with nonuniform clientele whose problems are not well understood (for example, schools in changing neighborhoods, psychiatric agencies)
4. Those with nonuniform clientele whose problems are well understood (for example, a programmed learning school).

Clearly boredom will be more of a problem for employees in type II organizations. Employees will probably be highly frustrated in types I and III. Type IV should pose technical challenges.

TANGIBILITY OF PRODUCT. Another approach to viewing, studying, or categorizing organizations is to classify them in terms of the degree to which the purpose of the organization is profit/product, and the degree to which it is human services. This could be stated as the degree to which goals are tangible, precise, and easily measurable; or less tangible, imprecise, and more difficult to measure. Here are three examples: 124

Auto, TV, washing-machine manufacturers	— Precise goals; tangible product; profit motive; easy to measure exactly the extent to which goals are being achieved.
Hospital, opera society	— Fairly precise goals; not-too-tangible product; must keep accounts in the black; not so easy to measure how adequately goals are achieved or relationship of goals to fiscal accounting.
School, university, museum, welfare agency	— Rather general goals, largely behavioral in nature; product is not very tangible and not easy to quantify; more emphasis on quality, but that remains intangible and difficult to measure, isolate, attribute cause and effect.

35

125 **IS THAT ALL THERE IS?** Such typologies can illuminate certain features of organizations and alert us to possible implications and problems. However, they oversimplify and presume too much. Organizations are too complex to be adequately described with a few concepts. For example, in what respects does the public benefit more from police departments than police officers do? Do students benefit more from school than administrators or teachers? Are employees the only ones who benefit from labor unions? Is it accurate to assume that parents of public school students have nothing to say about where their children will attend school when we know that they often move, pay tuition to another district, or send children to private school? Also, schools do have some control; for example, they expel some students, "push out" others, send some to special agencies, and use informal influence to recruit particularly favored students.

126 Moreover, it is misleading to place schools, hospitals, churches, and the like in any single category. Wide variations exist within each of these types of organizations. For example, the level of moral involvement within even a single factory is likely to be higher for professionals in the research department than for assembly-line workers. Or consider how the many differences between a one-room schoolhouse and a public school in New York City would affect how "schools" are categorized. Moreover, although in some schools the students might be morally committed to the goals (such as in some elite suburban schools), other schools are far more utilitarian. They try to bargain for the student's attention by offering a sports program, no homework, easy grades, or jobs in local industries. Also the teachers in utilitarian-type schools are less highly committed to their teaching careers. Discipline, as well as other problems, and dropout rates among students in utilitarian-type high schools reflect a high degree of alienation or, at best, calculative involvement.

127 This criticism does not mean that the typologies are not useful. They help explain and provide insights into the variations among hospitals, schools, churches, etc. For example, in one study it was found that there is variability in compliance patterns among different levels of schools (Hodgkins and Herriott, 1970). A normative relationship, indicated in Etzioni's typology, was found between teachers and principals at the lower grades of elementary schools, where teachers participated more in staff decisions and were more closely supervised. At the upper grades, the schools were utilitarian.

WHAT DIFFERENCE DOES THE SOCIAL ENVIRONMENT MAKE?

128 Perhaps we have given the impression that organizations exist in a vacuum, and, of course, that is not so. Organizations are shaped by, and in turn affect, their environments. In fact the way an organization is organized can make a big difference to each of us as citizens and as members. We have noted that excessive standardization might reduce our ability to gain access to the organization or might reduce its responsiveness to our wishes as citizens. Low-income people, in particular, often have difficulty with large service organizations (Sjoberg, Brymer, and Farris, 1966). They generally lack knowledge about how to manipulate bureaucratic rules and procedures to their advantage and they usually deal with people at the lower levels of the organization who are most constrained by the rules. Some authors believe lower-class clients have special difficulties in dealing with people on the impersonal level—a level characteristic of bureaucratic service organizations. All of these characteristics reinforce feelings of alienation among lower-class people.

129 Conversely, the social environment shapes organizations. For example, service organizations that serve low-income people often have less qualified staffs than those that serve

wealthier clientele. One study suggested that junior high schools serving lower-class students make greater use of rules governing teacher behavior than schools in middle-class neighborhoods. This illustrates how organizations adapt to their local communities (Anderson, 1968).

The Problem of Balance

Organizations must balance a delicate relationship with the local community. If they become too autonomous, they run the risk of losing touch with their constituencies which pay the cost of their services or products. On the other hand, organizations need some autonomy. For example, schools need some autonomy from parents in order to maintain standards of objectivity in dealing with students, determining curriculum and instructional procedures, setting learning expectations, evaluating, and grading students. 130

How is this balance maintained? Various "linkage mechanisms" are used which, in schools, include visiting teachers, neighborhood centers, Parent-Teacher Association, voluntary workers from the local community, and the like. One study indicated that where citizens are already closely involved with a school (as is the case in some middle-class neighborhoods), the school tries to increase the social distance (Litwak and Meyer, 1974). A teacher in such a school would not be expected to work closely with parents. On the other hand, where social distance is presumably already high, as in some lower-class neighborhoods, the schools use more initiative to reduce the social distance. A teacher might be expected to visit homes, for example. 131

However, it seems unrealistic to expect that an organization will voluntarily seek more contact with citizens unless it does not have to give up control. When organizations voluntarily reach out, they are not necessarily extending opportunities to citizens to influence their policies. More likely, they are attempting to coopt the citizens or otherwise extend their own control. 132

Beyond the Local Community

Sometimes the local community is not the main force acting on organizations. Organizations are also affected by regional variations and national influences. One study showed that schools in the more modernized regions of the country had higher proportions of teachers with master's degrees, and higher academic achievement by students (Herriott and Hodgkins, 1973). Also, schools in the less modernized parts of the country, for example in the rural south, change more slowly than schools in other parts of the country (Corwin, 1973). There is a strong sense of fundamentalism or tradition in the less modernized regions. However, while fundamentalist values do help to protect the less modernized schools from unplanned change, these schools seem to be more vulnerable to change deliberately introduced by new teacher-interns in the Teacher Corps than schools in the modernized areas (Edelfelt, 1974). The latter schools had more effective structural defenses against the interns, such as a centralized administration, strong teacher organizations, and better trained teachers. 133

What determines whether employees are more influenced by local, regional, or national influences? It depends partly on the other organizations with which employees are associated. A junior high school is associated with other schools in the system—a variety of "feeder" elementary schools from which it recruits students, one or more high schools to which it promotes students, and the like. In addition, it must deal with community advisory groups, tax groups interested in school bond issues, firms that employ its graduates, courts, social work agencies, police, and many other organizations in a community. 134

37

135   Many of these organizations are locally based, but others are based outside the community—accrediting and testing agencies, textbook publishers, government agencies, teacher training institutions, professional organizations, and more. The fact that a school is tied into such nationwide networks often acts as a conservative force on education. For example, if teachers in a school want to make a major change, they may run into problems with the accrediting agency, or the proper textbooks may be unavailable, or the teachers may be untrained for this particular innovation (Wayland, 1964). On the other hand, these national networks sometimes have deliberately promoted change. One such network, consisting of the National Science Foundation, committees of university professors, textbook publishers, and private agencies, induced a significant change by introducing modern mathematics into most schools in this country (Clark, 1965). The Teacher Corps is another example of a loose network of organizations affiliated for the purpose of improving teacher training (Corwin, 1973). In sum, the ability of members of a local organization to respond to local community influences will depend partly on the number and influence of organizations in its network that are based *outside* the community.

136   The cosmopolitan background of the members is another factor that will influence an organization's responsiveness to the local community. Organizations staffed primarily by people from the local community probably will be more responsive to community pressures than if the staff comes predominantly from outside the region. One study indicated that superintendents who were promoted from inside devoted most of their activities to enforcing existing rules and did not attempt to modify or redefine the commitments of the school system (Carlson, 1962). Those who were hired from the outside, on the other hand, attempted to make major changes, such as introducing kindergartens or school social workers. This does not mean that the outsider is the cause of these changes, because often a school board hires outsiders only when it is ready for a change.

137   Finally, some organizations are less vulnerable to pressures than others because they have developed effective strategies to resist local influence. For example, schools often have been able to coopt community groups, such as the PTA, which can serve as a "front" to support proposals that a principal alone could not get the school board to approve (Corwin, 1967). Superintendents sometimes are able to coopt their school boards because (a) board members often do not have identifiable constituencies that watch the board members and make their desires known, and (b) the superintendent has more time, information, and experience to deal with matters, causing boards to defer to superintendents (Kerr, 1964).

HOW CAN A PERSON DEAL WITH ORGANIZATIONS?

138   Until now we have been concentrating on how different types of organizations function. Understanding this helps us to explain and perhaps even to predict events and problems that would otherwise seem puzzling. However, there are times when simple understanding is not enough. We feel compelled to take action. What options are open to us as individuals and as members of the organization?

Personal Coping Strategies

139   Each individual has a choice of strategies in dealing with an organization. Depending on whether the individual subscribes to the goals of the organization and/or its procedures, he or she may choose as follows (Merton, 1957):

- To *conform,* that is, to subscribe to both goals and procedures
- To *innovate,* that is, to subscribe to the goals but reject the procedures

- To *conform ritualistically,* that is, to reject the goals but conform to the procedures
- To *retreat*, that is, to reject both the goals and the procedures
- To *rebel,* that is, to reject both goals and procedures and attempt to substitute a new set of goals and procedures.

The strategy that one chooses for a particular situation depends upon a variety of considerations in addition to one's personality, including social pressures, status within the organization, options to leave the organization, and sophistication about how organizations operate. [140]

Social pressures are the feelings that a person has based on the actions, attitudes, and expectations of one's friends or fellow workers. The importance of social pressure was illustrated in a study of a teachers' strike in New York City (Cole, 1969). Whether or not a teacher went out on strike depended largely on whether the teacher's friends supported the strike. Even individuals who were not personally predisposed to support the strike did strike if most of their friends supported it. [141]

Status is the deference and respect granted to a person by his fellow workers based not solely on one's actual position but often on a person's willingness to take risks. People at the bottom of the hierarchy have little to lose and much to gain from taking risks involved in innovation or rebellion. Also, people at the very top of the organization can afford to take some risks; not only are they expected to exert leadership, but also, because of their high status, they can afford to be wrong occasionally without loss of face. The person in the middle of the hierarchy is in a more tenuous position with a great deal to lose. He or she is likely to conform (Blau, 1964). [142]

Options are the choices a person feels are open. Some people have become very dependent on the organizations that employ them perhaps because they are too old or their skills are too obsolete to secure a comparable job elsewhere, or perhaps they are reluctant to leave their friends, neighbors, or colleagues. But other people have a variety of job options and are willing to move if necessary. Such options provide a margin for taking some risks (Corwin, 1976). [143]

To summarize, a person with very few options, who occupies a middle-level position within his or her organization and who is under pressure from friends and colleagues to conform, is likely to conform. The person with more options, who is in a position at the top or near the bottom of the organization and whose friends and colleagues support nonconformity, is in a position to innovate or rebel. People with some of these characteristics, but not others, probably will retreat. [144]

SOPHISTICATION ABOUT ORGANIZATIONS. Aside from an individual being in a position to take risks, there is still a question about the strategy that will be most effective. It is on the question of strategy that individuals often misjudge the situation. In a study of early cycles of the Teacher Corps, it was found that the more rebellious the interns were, the less the schools changed (Corwin, 1973). The rebellious interns probably would have been more effective in implementing change if they had analyzed the situation, including their own position in it, and if they had a clearer understanding about how organizations do change. Let us consider innovation strategies in more detail. [145]

HOW DO ORGANIZATIONS CHANGE?

Probably most people would agree that no matter how well their organization is now operating, it could be improved. Some individuals or groups are more intent on [146] changing their organization than others. Some reformists advocate wholesale change; others prefer a step-by-step, piecemeal plan. Some reformists are patient and adopt an evolutionary perspective; others are impatient and advocate radical methods. In effect, each of these groups operates with different theories about organizations and with different theories about how they change. The fact is that most reform today must be put into effect by and through organized groups and, therefore, any reform effort will be subject to the forces and constraints that govern complex social systems. Before any of us tries reform, we should first become students of organizational change, which ultimately means students of organization.

Is This the Moment?

147 Reform is an idea whose time has come. That is, change takes place as part of a larger process and cannot be implemented until the situation is ripe—until certain conditions are present. In one model of change, those conditions can be seen in stages:

Stage 1: The ability of an organization as presently structured lags behind new demands made of it, that is, behind public expectations.

Stage 2: A crisis develops from this strain between the public demand and the organization's ability to deliver; and leaders, who in normal times are under conservative pressures, are expected to innovate.

Stage 3: Groups outside the organization provide incentives for and pressure on the organization to change. Eventually they form coalitions with progressive members of the organization who oppose the conservative leadership. This outside support gives the inside challengers extra leverage against conservative opposition.

Stage 4: Resistance takes the form of superficial change, disinterest, sabotage, piecemeal acceptance, or rejection of larger plans and adding to existing programs rather than transforming them.

Stage 5: Various forms of the innovation evolve, most become extinct or indistinguishable from existing forms; but through natural selection, an optimal match occurs between some hybrids and local conditions.

Stage 6: Once established, the innovation becomes routinized and subject to the same forces that created the need for it. Most of today's practices are yesterday's innovations.

How to Do It

148 Writers have advocated a variety of approaches to changing organizations (Corwin, 1973, pp. 248-56). For example, it has been postulated that an organization can be more easily changed:

- if it is invaded by liberal, creative, and unconventional outsiders with fresh perspectives . . .
- if those outsiders are exposed to creative, competent, flexible socialization agents . . .
- if it is staffed by young, flexible, supportive, and competent boundary personnel or "gatekeepers" . . .
- if it is structurally complex and decentralized (i.e., employees participate in decisions) . . .

40

- if it has outside funds to provide the organizational slack necessary to lessen the cost of innovation . . .
- if its members have positions that are sufficiently secure and protected from the status risks involved in change . . .
- if it is located in a changing, modern, urbanized setting where it is in close cooperation with a coalition of other cosmopolitan organizations that can supplement its skills and resources . . . (p. 255).

It should be clear that organizational reform is a complicated process that should not ₁₄₉ be undertaken without serious study and reflection. A combination of approaches is required in most cases. We should be wary of strategists who promise simple solutions to complicated problems. Poorly planned strategies can easily backfire. For example, the attempt to use Teacher Corps interns as "change agents" (via the replacement strategy) in the early cycles did not work:

> The attempt to unite the change-agent roles with the apprenticeship system placed the interns in a precarious position between two powerful organizations. They were representatives of the outside organization in the schools but could count on little direct support from remote university professors; also they were directly supervised by defensive teachers. Sensing this resistance to them, and often finding the schools conservative toward change, in most programs a vocal minority of interns resorted to confrontation tactics. However, the conflict theory of change presumes a balance of power which did not exist in this case. As inexperienced newcomers to the profession, still in training and temporarily assigned to schools under direct supervision of experienced teachers, the interns could not gain leverage within the schools—even though, ironically, these very characteristics enabled them to maintain the autonomy which encouraged them to take risks involved in promoting change. Nor did the interns constitute a sufficiently critical mass in any of the schools to provide power from numbers or to promote the development of a strong peer group. They were so outnumbered and overwhelmed by the structural defenses available to the school administrators and teachers that the schools were able to neutralize their efforts. Indeed, the interns' militancy gave the teachers little latitude to compromise without jeopardizing their authority, which created a win-lose situation. Teachers retaliated by completely withdrawing their support for interns' proposals. Thus, while some change accompanied conflict, the fact that interns had little leverage with which to wage a successful conflict helps explain the negative correlation between technological change and the proportion of liberal arts interns in the program (Corwin, 1973, p. 278).

WHERE DOES THIS LEAVE US?

In these pages, we have been able to provide only a brief overview of perspectives on ₁₅₀ organizations. We have tried to gear our discussion to the typical person who has dealt with many types of organizations during the course of his or her life, but who has not had an opportunity to think systematically about the assumptions used in coping with them. The concepts and principles introduced here represent only a modest beginning, but we hope that the reader's curiosity has been aroused and that he or she appreciates the potential of such study for life and career. Most of all, we hope that the reader will join us in extending and applying this knowledge to everyday life.

Ideally, a student of organizations will be able to make more deliberate, informed, ₁₅₁ and constructive decisions. This first volume is designed to assist such students in beginning that process. Toward this end, we have added some references, abstracts, and a bibliography to facilitate exploration and, if the reader would like to try writing a case study, we have provided some suggestions. This is the first, an overview volume, of a series of volumes that explore in great depth many of the issues raised here.

REFERENCES

Anderson, J.G. *Bureaucracy in Education.* Baltimore, Md.: Johns Hopkins Press, 1968.

Argyris, C. *Personality and Organization.* New York: Harper and Row, 1957.

Bennis, W.G., and P.E. Slater. *The Temporary Society.* New York: Harper and Row, 1968.

Blau, P.M. *Exchange and Power in Social Life.* New York: Wiley, 1964.

Blau, P.M. "Theories of Organizations." In D.L. Sills, ed., *International Encyclopedia of Social Science* Vol. 11. New York: Macmillan, 1968, pp. 297-304.

Blau, P.M. "A Formal Theory of Differentiation in Organizations." *American Sociological Review* 35 (1970): 201-18.

Blau, P.M., and R. Scott. *Formal Organizations.* San Francisco: Chandler, 1962.

Caplow, T. *Principles of Organizations.* New York: Harcourt, Brace and World, 1964.

Carlson, R.O. "Environmental Constraints and Organizational Consequences: The Public School and Its Clients." In D.E. Griffiths, ed., *Behavioral Science and Educational Administration.* 63rd Yearbook of the National Society for the Study of Education, Part II. Chicago: National Society for the Study of Education, 1964, pp. 262-76.

Clark, B.R. "Interorganizational Patterns in Education." *Administrative Science Quarterly* 10 (1965): 224-37.

Cole, S. "Teachers' Strike: A Study of the Conversion of Predisposition into Action." *American Journal of Sociology* 74 (1969):506-20.

Corwin, R.G. "Professional Persons in Public Organizations." *Educational Administration Quarterly* 1 (1965):1-22.

Corwin, R.G. "Education and the Sociology of Complex Organizations." In D. Hansen and J. Gerstl, eds., *On Education: Sociological Perspectives.* New York: Wiley, 1967, pp. 156-223.

Corwin, R.G. *Militant Professionalism: A Study of Organizational Conflict in High Schools.* New York: Appleton-Century-Crofts, 1970.

Corwin, R.G. *Reform and Organizational Survival: The Teacher Corps as an Instrument of Educational Change.* New York: Wiley-Interscience, 1973.

Corwin, R.G. "Models of Educational Organizations." In F. Kerlinger and J. Carroll, eds., *Review of Research in Education.* Itasca, Ill.: F.E. Peacock, 1974, pp. 247-95.

Corwin, R.G. "Innovation in Organizations: The Case of Schools." *Sociology of Education* 48 (1975): 1-37.

Corwin, R.G. "Implementation Problems: The Social Costs of Change." In R. Jacobs, ed., *Flexible Education for the Health Professions.* New York: Wiley, forthcoming.

Corwin, R.G. "The Organizational Context of School Board-Teacher Conflict." In P.J. Cistone, ed., *School-Board-Research: Main Lines of Inquiry.* Lexington, Mass.: D.C. Heath, 1975.

Corwin, R.G., M.J. Taves, and J.E. Haas. "Professional Disillusionment." *Nursing Research* 10 (1961): 141-44.

Corwin, R.G., and T.C. Wagenaar. "Interaction Between Service Organizations and Their Publics: An Exploratory Analysis of Boundary Spanning Relations." Unpublished paper, Ohio State University, 1975.

Dahrendorf, R. *Class and Class Conflict in Industrial Society.* Stanford, Calif.: Stanford University Press, 1959.

Edelfelt, R.A. and R.G. Corwin. *Lessons from the Teacher Corps.* Washington, D.C.: National Education Association, 1974.

Etzioni, A. *A Comparative Analysis of Complex Organizations.* New York: Free Press, 1961.

Etzioni, A. *Modern Organizations.* Englewood Cliffs, N.J.: Prentice-Hall, 1964.

Gerth, H.H., and C.W. Mills (trans. and eds.). *From Max Weber: Essays in Sociology.* New York: Oxford University Press, 1946.

Gouldner, A.W. "Red Tape as a Social Problem." In R.K. Merton, A.P. Gray, B. Hockey, and H.C. Selvin, eds., *Reader in Bureaucracy.* Glencoe, Ill.: Free Press, 1952, pp. 410-18.

Gouldner, A.W. *Patterns of Industrial Bureaucracy.* Glenco, Ill.: Free Press, 1954.

Gouldner, A.W. "Organizational Analysis." In R.K. Merton, L. Bloom, and L.S. Cottrell, Jr., eds., *Sociology Today.* New York: Basic Books, 1959, pp. 400-28.

Haas, J.E., and T.E. Drabek. *Complex Organizations: A Sociological Perspective.* New York: Macmillan, 1973.

Havighurst, R.J. *The Public Schools of Chicago.* Chicago: The Board of Education, 1964.

Henderson, A.M., and T. Parsons (trans.). *Max Weber: The Theory of Social and Economic Organization.* Glencoe, Ill.: Free Press, 1947.

Herriott, R.E., and B.J. Hodgkins. *The Environment of Schooling: Formal Education as an Open Social System.* Englewood Cliffs, N.J.: Prentice-Hall, 1973.

Heydebrand, W.U., ed. *Comparative Organizations: The Results of Empirical Research.* Englewood Cliffs, N.J.: Prentice-Hall, 1973.

Hodgkins, B.J., and R.E. Herriott. "Age-Grade Structure, Goals, and Compliance in the School: An Organizational Analysis." *Sociology of Education* 43 (1970):90-105.

Katz, D., and R.L. Kahn. "Organizations and the System Concept." In *Social Psychology of Organizations.* New York: Wiley, 1966, pp. 14-29.

Kaufman, B. *Up the Down Staircase.* New York: Avon, 1966.

Kerr, N.D. "The School Board as an Agency of Legitimation." *Sociology of Education* 38 (1964): 34-59.

Lane, W.R., R.G. Corwin and W.G. Monahan. *Foundations of Educational Administration: A Behavioral Analysis.* New York: Macmillan, 1967.

Lazarsfeld, P., and H. Menzel. "On the Relation Between Individual and Collective Properties." In A. Etzioni, ed., *A Sociological Reader on Complex Organizations,* 2nd ed. New York: Holt, Rinehart and Winston, 1969, pp. 499-516.

Litwak, E. "Models of Bureaucracy Which Permit Conflict." *American Journal of Sociology* 67 (1961):177-85.

Litwak, E., and H.J. Meyer. *School, Family, and Neighborhood: The Theory and Practice of School-Community Relationships.* New York: Columbia University Press, 1974.

Lortie, D.C. "The Balance of Control and Autonomy in Elementary School Teaching." In A. Etzioni, ed., *The Semi-Professions and Their Organizations:Teachers, Nurses, Social Workers.* New York: Free Press, 1969, pp. 1-53.

Merton, R.K. "Bureaucratic Structure and Personality." In R.K. Merton, ed., *Social Theory and Social Structure.* Glencoe, Ill.: Free Press, 1957, pp. 195-206.

Peabody, R.L. *Organizational Authority.* New York: Atherton; Englewood Cliffs, N.J.: Prentice-Hall, 1964.

Perrow, C. *Organizational Analysis: A Sociological View.* Belmont, Calif.: Brooks/Cole, 1970.

Rogers, D. *110 Livingston Street.* New York: Random House, 1968.

Sjoberg, G., R. Brymer, and B. Farris. "Bureaucracy and the Lower Class." *Sociology and Social Research* 50 (1966):325-37.

Wayland, S.R. "Structural Features of American Education as Basic Factors in Innovation." In M. Miles, ed., *Innovations in Education.* New York: Columbia University, Teachers College Press, 1964, pp. 587-614.

Wouk, H. *The Caine Mutiny.* Garden City, N.Y.: Doubleday, 1951.

Part III

Organizations in Action

Part I of this book described the assumptions, rationale, and objectives behind the instructional process suggested for presenting the materials relevant to studying organizations. In Part II, Ronald Corwin and Roy Edelfelt defined and discussed some key concepts necessary for understanding organizations. The purpose of this section is to describe some possible activities that might help familiarize participants with the concepts in Part III and encourage them to test and apply their knowledge. A summary of the suggested activities is followed by suggested procedures and other information needed to carry out each exercise.

The instructor should select activities in the order that best suits participant level of awareness and the instructional purpose. Generally, the intention is to present activities so that the participant begins with what he or she already knows, then meets new concepts and explores some of those concepts in depth. The instructor or the participants will probably want to modify or add to the list of activities offered.

SUMMARY OF ACTIVITIES

1. Draw an Organization: An introductory exercise.
2. Life in Organizations: Reading about and discussing organizations.
3. Terry Trevors: Applying what has been learned about organizations to a case study.
4. *Bridge on the River Kwai:* Applying what has been learned to a feature-length film.
5. Vignettes: Exploring some concepts in greater detail.
6. Up Against the Organization: Relating learning about organizations to personal experience.
7. Research: Studying independently. Some references to be used for independent study appear in Appendix A, Bibliography, and at the end of Part II.

Activity 1—
Draw an Organization

The purpose of this activity is to assist participants as they begin to develop an understanding of organizations. It is assumed that everyone has some knowledge of organizations from direct experiences, whether those experiences were positive or negative.

Participants are directed first to recall some of the organizations to which they have belonged and to consider what they did as members, what the organization did, how it got started, and how it operated. They should begin to imagine how they might graphically represent the organization they have selected. Consideration of the following steps may be helpful:

- Draw an organization you have been considering. (The instructor should provide chart paper and marking pens.) Use pictures, words, or symbols if you like. **Do not** draw an organization chart. **Do** try to include what you feel are important elements of the organization. (10 minutes)

- Show your drawing to others in the group. Explain what the drawing depicts. Group members may ask questions to help you further define the organization you have described. (5 minutes for each participant)
- Review the drawings of each group member, formulate a definition of organization, and note common characteristics of organizations that the participants have drawn. Each group will complete the chart below to summarize its findings. (20 minutes)

```
An organization is:




Common characteristics:


```

- Post the drawings and the chart so that other groups may see them.

Participants will proceed next to the reading of Part II. They will match their definition and the list of common characteristics with those provided in Part II. After reading, group members may revise their original definition and may add to the list of characteristics.

Activity 2—
Life in Organizations

Once participants' interest in studying organizations has been stimulated and they have developed their own definitions and list of characteristics, they will be ready to read Part II, "Life in Organizations." On the first reading they should locate the authors' definition of organization and compare it to their own. They should see how many characteristics they identified as common to all organizations are also described by Corwin and Edelfelt. On the basis of their reading, students should be encouraged to review, revise, and add to the charts they developed during the first activity, "Draw an Organization."

After reading "Life in Organizations," participants will be engaging in various activities described in this section. Following each activity participants should be encouraged to review the appropriate sections of Part II. The following chart on concepts will help both participants and instructors relate their reading in Part II to the activities they undertake.

46

LIFE IN ORGANIZATIONS

MAJOR CONCEPTS
(WHERE THEY ARE LOCATED IN PART I; WHERE THEY ARE EXPLORED IN PART III)

Concepts	Part II-Paragraph Number	Draw an Organization	Terry Trevors	Bridge on the River Kwai	Vignettes	Up Against the Organization	Abstracts of Selected Readings
1. Reasons for studying organizations	1-21					x	
2. Complexities of belonging to organizations	22-27		x			x	x
3. Professional employees, work group organizations	18-19 25-27		x	x	x		x
4. Definition of organization, formal, informal	28-32	x	x	x	x		x
5. Organization goals	33-34		x	x			
6. Social systems	35-40			x			
7. Bureaucracy	41-49	x	x	x			
8. Organization theory	50-56						x
9. Approaches to studying organizations	57-64						x
10. Individual and the organization	65-67		x	x		x	
11. Key features of organizations	68-70	x	x	x			
Vertical dimensions	71	x	x	x			
— Power	72		x	x			
— Authority	73		x	x			x
— Responsibility	74		x	x			
— Prestige	75			x			
— Esteem	76		x	x			
— Competence	77		x	x			
— Status inconsistency	78-81			x	x		
— Emulation	82, 83		x	x	x		
— Delegation	84			x			
— Slippage	85-86			x			
Horizontal dimensions	87				x		
— Zones of autonomy	88-90						x
— Power	91			x			
Integrating dimensions	92, 103	x					
— Standardization	93-98		x	x			
— Direct supervision	99		x	x			
— Mutual adjustment	100						
— Scheduling	101						
— Reporting	102		x				
12. Kinds of organizations	104						
Models	105, 109, 110, 112-14				x		
— Rational model	106-107			x			
— Organic model	108						
— Middle ground model	111						
Typologies	115, 125-27		x				
— Beneficiary	116		x				
— Means of control	117-19		x				
— Membership	120-21		x				
— Techniques	122-23		x				
— Tangibility of product	124		x				
13. Social environment	128-37		x				x
14. Conformity	137		x				
15. Coping strategies	138-45		x			x	
16. Organization change	146-49				x	x	x

Activity 3—
Terry Trevors: A Sequential Case Study

Concepts and ideas often can be effectively illustrated and illuminated through case studies. Portraying some concrete circumstances surrounding a problem serves as a common ground for discussion; and because participants are not directly affected by the case, they can learn from it in nonthreatening ways. They also can gain some perspective on their own problems as they try their hand at writing an account of cases with which they are familiar.

The case selected for discussion here has been included for illustrative purposes. It is not necessarily the best case for the purpose, and the reader may wish to find or write others that are more appropriate. Nor would we suggest that our analysis is the only one possible. Each analyst will bring a personal perspective. What is important is that in the process of reflecting on a case, abstract concepts and ideas take on additional dimensions of meaning and significance.

SUGGESTIONS FOR USE OF THE CASE

"Terry Trevors" is a case study that gives the participant an excellent opportunity to identify characteristics of organizations and organizational norms and to examine role conflict and coping strategies. The case is sequential and contains three parts (A, B, and C) which are distributed and discussed individually. Because participants review one part of the case at a time, they are able to discuss the problem and suggest alternative solutions and then compare their responses to those of the characters in the case. The sequential approach allows participants to consider only small amounts of material at a time. Some suggestions for ways in which the case may be used are described below. The suggestions are followed by a review and analysis of the case and a copy of the case study.

- The instructor might begin by reviewing the case study and the analysis in order to plan its introduction to participants and to plan the discussions that will follow each part of the case. If possible, we suggest that discussions be in small groups of 8-12 people. Participants should know that the case represents one technique for applying the knowledge they have been acquiring. They should be encouraged to examine Terry's problem from an organizational as well as a personal point of view.

- The following procedure is one possible way to work through the case:
  1. Distribute Part A. Read, discuss and identify the problems illustrated.
  2. Distribute Part B. (It may be more appropriate to distribute and read parts A and B before any discussion.) Read and discuss parts A and B, using the following questions:
     - How would you describe the problem(s) in this case? What organizational characteristics are contributing to the problem(s)?
     - What additional questions would you raise to obtain the information necessary to understand this situation?
     - In what ways could this problem best be dealt with?
     - What strategies could Terry use to cope with the problem? What would you do in this situation? Why?
     - What are the sources of pressure acting on the individuals and groups in the case?

48

- What are the key characteristics of the organizations involved?
- What organizational norms are in play?
3. Distribute part C. Read and discuss part C, using the following questions as a guide:
   - Does your analysis of the situation change with the additional information? How?
   - How would you describe the problems now? What organizational characteristics are contributing to the problems?
   - What strategies could Terry use to cope with the problem? What would you do now?
   - What additional information would you need to completely analyze the problem?
   - Do you perceive Terry to be a male or a female? How does your perception affect your analysis?
4. Summarize the case.

The instructor may choose to follow this procedure with some variations. Parts A and B might be distributed before the group meets to discuss the case, and each member may prepare an initial analysis. When the group meets, the discussion might be started by several participants, each presenting his or her initial analysis. The other group members may then join the discussion.

If appropriate to the flow of instruction, participants may simply receive the case one part at a time in class. After discussing parts A and B, they might enjoy preparing a written projection of what is likely to occur in part C. Upon receipt of part C they would compare their responses to the real case, and then proceed to a discussion of the questions provided.

To achieve some measure of closure, it will be important to generalize about the analysis of the case. The group may refer to the list of major concepts as an aid. Either the instructor, the participants, or both may choose to offer the concluding statements which may include drawing comparisons with the analyses of other case studies, films, or simulations. References to concepts developed in Part II should also be encouraged. (The group may be informed that this case study is true and is still pending in the courts in Washington State.)

Terry Trevors—Part A

by Dale Troxel

Terry Trevors was a social studies teacher, widely reputed to be the most liberal of the more than 300 teachers in the community senior high. For five years Terry had been teaching in the school, whose administration and faculty, like the community itself, were notably conservative. However, throughout this period, Terry's liberal views were generally considered harmless and were tolerated in degrees ranging from good-natured to grudging. In fact, Terry was twice elected by colleagues to the board of directors of the local education association. Before emotions in the community became heated, Terry could have remained known as merely another "warmed-over New Dealer" and retired uneventfully in the year 2000.

In November 1965, however, Terry was elected vice-chairperson of the county chapter of the American Civil Liberties Union (ACLU), and from November 1966 to

November 1969 served as chairperson. As an ACLU official, Terry became involved in a number of controversial issues that were common to America's general unrest at that period, and gradually became a figure on whom local reaction to societal unrest focused.

The following issues were among those in which Terry as an ACLU official became involved with the school system from an adversary position:

- Can students be required to salute the American flag? (The United States Supreme Court had ruled in 1943 that students could not be required to do so.)
- Can a school dress code be imposed other than for reasons of health or safety? (As a result of an opinion rendered by the state attorney general, the school district abandoned this practice.)
- Can a public school direct a student to remove a peace medallion? (This issue arose a few weeks after the Supreme Court had ruled that only in situations where a button would substantially disrupt classes could a student be required to remove it.)
- Can a public school expel a pregnant student who has been married for 10 months?
- Can a public school confiscate a school petition that is causing no disruption?
- Can a public school prohibit distribution of underground newspapers?
- Should the principal of a public high school pressure a teacher to withdraw an invitation to the local ACLU chairperson to speak about the organization to an after-school extracurricular group?

Terry handled several of these matters confidentially so that only a few of them became known to the general public. Some were not even known to the school board. However, although they were minor issues, each of them generated hostility from at least certain members of the school system and the community.

Two other ACLU issues that Terry became involved in generated publicly intense controversies that focused a great deal of attention on Terry personally. The first instance was when Terry publicly defended the contention of the ACLU that adult sale and use of marijuana should be legal. The second instance centered around the general question of religious practice in the public schools and involved such conventions of the local school system as the following:

- sponsoring and conducting baccalaureate exercises of a religious nature in violation of a 1962 opinion of the state attorney general;
- maintaining a student chaplain in contradiction of the opinion of another attorney general that such chaplains violate the federal constitution;
- continuing religious standards for recipients of two honorary student awards and inquiring into the religious beliefs of students before determining eligibility for those awards.

Terry raised these religious issues in the spring of 1966 and again in the summer of 1967, causing intensely emotional arguments among the men and women of the high school faculty. When the ACLU threatened to bring suit in June 1968, the opposition to Terry's ACLU activities reached its height. Within a single week, Terry was denounced by the local Chamber of Commerce, the mayor, and the president of the ministerial association. The local newspaper, which was generally hostile to the national, state, and local purposes of the ACLU, carried about 70 articles and letters regarding this controversy. The school district continued to enjoy the support of the majority of the articulate public, although the means by which it had handled the situation had been referred to as "devious" by several respected leaders. When confronted by the ACLU, the school abandoned the practices in question rather than face a lawsuit. From that point forward, however, Terry was unpopular. The principal made veiled threats concerning Terry's teaching contract and appeared to have strong backing from the superintendent of schools.

When questioned by colleagues at the high school concerning the ACLU activities and the possibility that they conflicted with the continuation of a successful career in teaching, Terry replied, "My political views are my own affair, and I have a right guaranteed under the Constitution of the United States to continue expressing them."

Terry Trevors—Part B

Terry Trevors was a high school social studies teacher who became well known in the community as a result of a number of controversies centering around the American Civil Liberties Union (ACLU), of which Terry was a local officer. Terry's personal relationships with both male and female students in the high school were generally friendly, and it was not uncommon for students to visit Terry's house. The Winter 1969 issue of the *Canadian Education Quarterly,* a magazine about schools, carried an underground article by Jerry Farber, which was entitled "The Student as Nigger." It denounced American education in very coarse and radical language. After receiving copies from a local college student in 1969, Terry permitted any high school student who asked for it to have a copy. In conversation with a colleague, Terry expressed the opinion that there was no reason for concern about distributing the essay because it was merely giving students reading material that they had requested, a perfectly defensible activity from either an individual or an educational point of view. Terry also expressed the opinion that having distributed copies of the article was "no big deal." The community disagreed.

The pressure on Terry personally was less intense than during a previous controversy that had occurred as a result of Terry's position regarding religion in the public schools, although more than 140 letters and articles concerning Terry and "The Student as Nigger" did appear in the local press. Some of the newspaper coverage led readers to conclude incorrectly that the Farber essay was part of Terry's classroom curriculum and/or that Terry was actually the author of the essay. The essay was commonly believed to reflect the views of both Terry and the ACLU. Terry was incensed at local opinion, having good reason to believe that at least four other teachers really did use "The Student as Nigger" as part of their curriculum without receiving such notoriety or criticism.

The majority of Terry's critics were neither fundamentalists nor members of the John Birch Society. However, the latter group, some of whose members had engaged in a local campaign the previous spring to publicize their idea that the ACLU was a communist organization, initiated and coordinated a movement to have Terry dismissed from the high school. An ad hoc group called the Civic Education Committee was formed. Its spokesman described it as conservative. Two of its 13 members were officers of the local chapter of the John Birch Society. The Civic Education Committee composed and circulated a petition urging that Terry be fired. It was signed by 500 members of the community, including a number of prominent local leaders.

Simultaneously, Terry was warned by a friend that the superintendent of schools had heard that large numbers of students were visiting Terry's home. The superintendent had made it apparent to colleagues that this practice was considered unethical.

As Terry's sixth year of teaching at the high school ended in June, the principal and the superintendent took the opportunity of a routine evaluation meeting to call attention to what were referred to as flaws in Terry's teaching. At least two-thirds of the conference pertained to Terry's outside activities, and the superintendent even stated that Terry's teaching would be considered much improved if Terry no longer took such an active part in public affairs. The principal asked if it was true that Terry was a communist and an officer of the ACLU, a local subversive organization.

In October 1969, Terry was banned from speaking at a neighboring high school; the principal of that school angrily explained the ban by saying, "My son in the Marine Corps does not approve of the ACLU, and I do not approve of the ACLU either." What Terry described as the "obvious absurdity of these comments and accusations" generally left Terry angry, but momentarily speechless. It seemed politically unwise to engage in an open argument with any of these people, and Terry could think of no other means of handling the situation.

"My relationships with my students mean a great deal to me," Terry explained to a friend in the education association. "If I back down now, I'll be violating everything I've been trying to teach them."

Terry Trevors—Part C

Terry Trevors was a high school social studies teacher who was investigated by the state education association for unethical conduct after distributing a controversial article called "The Student as Nigger" to all students who had asked for it. Terry had previously outraged some segments of the community by various activities as an officer of the local chapter of the American Civil Liberties Union (ACLU), and much of the community hoped that the investigation of unethical conduct would lead to Terry's dismissal.

The professional rights and responsibilities commission of the state education association conducted two days of hearings, interviewing 19 witnesses, only one of whom was called by Terry. At the conclusion of the investigation, the state report not only cleared Terry of the charge of unethical conduct, but also strongly criticized the administration of the school district for abridging Terry's academic freedom. Having been led to believe, by articles in the local newspaper, that the state investigation would put an end to the controversy over Terry's activities, much of the community reacted with intense anger when Terry was cleared of all charges. The school district needed little more to decide to terminate Terry's relationship with the school.

At the beginning of the following school year, a new principal was appointed to Terry's high school and arrived with instructions to "handle Terry firmly." These instructions soon became common knowledge among the teachers. Earlier, when the "nonissue" (in Terry's words) of "The Student as Nigger" had arisen, Terry had been instructed to no longer give anything to students that could be considered controversial and to submit weekly lesson plans, which were not required of other teachers.

Terry was treated differently from the rest of the teachers in a variety of other ways as well. It was common practice for teachers to be granted permission to speak to the Kiwanis Club during school hours. Terry had previously spoken with considerable effect, on the subject of academic freedom as it applied to Terry's own situation, to two business groups that met in the evening. When the Kiwanis requested that Terry address them in the afternoon, however, the principal would not grant Terry permission to leave.

Rumors began to circulate that Terry was a homosexual and, simultaneously, that Terry had been engaging in illicit activities with students of the opposite sex. Without

TERRY TREVORS

MAJOR CONCEPTS
- Formal organization
- Informal organization
- Role conflict
- Social environment
- Bureaucracy
- Vertical Dimension of Organizations—(Hierarchy)
    - Power
    - Authority
    - Competence
    - Esteem
- Integration of the Hierarchy
    - Emulation
    - Standardization
    - Supervision
    - Reporting
- Typologies
    - Service organization
    - Coersion
    - Membership
    - Technique
    - Tangibility of product

MAJOR CHARACTER
- Terry Trevors—A high school social studies teacher and ACLU officer

ORGANIZATIONS AND GROUPS
- School faculty
- School system
- Local education association
- American Civil Liberties Union (ACLU)
- Community
- Chamber of Commerce
- Ministerial association
- John Birch Society
- Civic Education Committee
- State education association
- Kiwanis Club

any apparent foundation, Terry was also accused of accepting bribes from students to postpone tests. In February the voters of the community turned down a special school levy, and the chairman of the school board cited Terry as one of the three reasons why this had occurred. A few months later it was announced that Terry's teaching contract would not be renewed for the following year. The school board cited 29 reasons, beginning with incompetence and ending with violation of an old state law requiring teachers to instruct their students in patriotism.

THE CASE IN BRIEF

Terry Trevors, a high school social studies teacher and an officer in the local chapter of the ACLU, was generally considered by school staff and students to be a good teacher. During six years as a teacher Terry became increasingly involved in a number of controversial issues ranging from the legalization of marijuana to academic freedom and individual student rights. As the community became more aware of Terry's activities and opinions, groups and individuals began to denounce Terry and to demand dismissal. Although the state education agency cleared Terry of the charge of unethical conduct, the public continued to be outraged and finally rejected a special school levy. The school system responded by blaming Terry in part, by treating Terry differently from other teachers, and by limiting opportunities available to Terry. Eventually unfounded rumors were circulated and it was announced that Terry's contract would not be renewed.

TERRY TREVORS—A CASE ANALYSIS*

What features of organizations are in play here? Since this case revolves around a central person, we can begin by considering Terry's position.

She* is an employee of the school district, and as a subordinate, she is subject to the directives and evaluations of the administration. This position places her at a power disadvantage in several respects. We saw how administrators were able to selectively enforce rules about the use of a controversial book to Terry's disadvantage, stop her public appearance, and ultimately, terminate her contract.

Nevertheless, her position within the formal hierarchy (reinforced with five years of experience) also affords her discretion over reading assignments, and she is sufficiently insulated and isolated from her supervisors that they were able to tolerate her until the publicity forced them to take action. She was not closely supervised, officials often deferring their actions until she came up for periodic review. And even when it had been decided to release her, she was not fired until the contract expired. But, of course, she was not entirely autonomous; her actions reflected upon the school.

For all their power, the administrators might have had less discretion in this situation than Terry. As agents of the school board, the central administration formulated, and then interpreted, policies to anticipate and reflect the views of influential, vocal segments of the community. The administration's instructions to the new principal made it clear that he was being watched and, in turn, was expected to emulate them by supervising Terry more closely. But even such deliberate control was not enough to counteract

---

*The name, Terry, is used by both men and women in our society. Was Terry a man or woman? We have found that many people assume that Terry is a male, which perhaps reflects a general stereotype about the passivity of women. We have chosen to believe that Terry is a woman. There may be value in discussing the case again on the assumption that Terry is a man, to see if the analysis changes.

immediately the natural organizational slack. Terry's actions had been tolerated for years because of this slack, and became controversial precisely because she chose to place her own interpretations on the policies. This was possible not only because she resisted the policies, but also because they were sufficiently ambiguous to allow for some interpretation. If we are to accept the report of the case writer as a complete picture, Terry seemed to be the only teacher at the school who was actually taking advantage of this slack.

But there is more to understanding Terry's position than her place in the formal hierarchy. What other positions does she hold, and how much protection and influence do they yield? First, she is highly esteemed by colleagues, and thus may have more support than is implied by the case writer. How do we know she is esteemed? Recall that she was twice elected by colleagues to an office in the local organization. She is more than an employee. She is a professional employee, and her professional status provides some leverage with the administration. While, unfortunately, we are not told how her colleagues felt about the administration's tactics (and the implication is that they are all conformists), isn't it likely that at least a few of these 300 teachers would be supportive of Terry? We can be sure that because they could be threatened the administration had to consider her colleagues' possible reactions as it dealt with Terry.

Terry also holds another position of esteem and influence as an officer in a civic organization, the ACLU. This outside organization provided her with support (the threatened ACLU law suit against the district) and was a source of her problems (ACLU's adversaries, such as the newspaper, turned on her).

So, Terry holds at least three types of positions—her position in the formal hierarchy of the school, which provides little power but some autonomy; her esteemed professional status in the teacher's organization; and her leadership position in a liberal civic organization. The fact that these positions are inconsistent in status left her with incompatible guides to appropriate actions. This exacerbated the role conflict.

So far, we have not said much about authority, or the right to use power. Where does authority reside in this situation? The whole problem arose because Terry challenged the formal authority structure. The administration, in turn, challenged the authority of the state education association by ignoring its report. Of course, each side claimed to have authority by appealing to public opinion, professional autonomy, the law, etc. It seems that authority is operative only while it is accepted by those subject to it, after which the outcome is decided by power—until appeals are made to a higher authority, such as the courts, that all parties do accept.

The administration took Terry's challenge as a sign of her alienation from the organization's values. While this was probably an accurate assessment as far as it goes, it is more accurate to say that she was committed to a competing outside value system. Consequently, normative appeals by the administration were not effective; nor is it likely that she could have been silenced with salary increases, a promotion, or other utilitarian rewards. There were only two options apparently open to the administration: to compete for her loyalty by making a place for someone like her, or to use coercive measures as it chose to do. But because coercion is ultimately incompatible with the normative style which schools try to use, the administration was forced to release Terry, thus acknowledging it did not have the means of controlling her.

This is probably why the administration tried to discredit Terry's personal morals. Terry was relying on the bureaucratic principle that one's career should be governed by technical competence and not by personal life style. Terry is probably an able teacher, and so the administration hoped to shift the issue to the explosive moral arena where she seemed more vulnerable in this conservative community (and where her colleagues may have been more reluctant to become involved).

This case dramatizes the fact that problems which seem to be internal to a school district are often actually fueled by organized groups in the outside environment. It is often not enough to understand only the internal workings of the organization. If the administration had ignored public opinion, it would have risked jeopardizing the district's budget and perhaps adversely have affected Terry's colleagues. In this political environment, compromising Terry's academic freedom may have seemed a necessary price to pay for protecting these other interests. At the same time, the administration might have been overreacting. Perhaps it could have protected Terry more. Individuals sometimes are sacrificed for "organizational justice," i.e., for the larger goals of the organization.

The state education association is another part of this external environment. This association transcended the local community and competed with the local school board for teachers' loyalties. But, although it put the weight of its professional authority behind Terry to help legitimate her position, the education association was not very effective. Why? We cannot be sure, but this was, afterall, a conflict of power. The prestige of this state organization was no match for the political forces at work in this local community, especially since its right to intervene in a local issue could be challenged. The education association might have been more effective had it chosen to use collective sanctions against the district, and conceivably that might have happened under certain circumstances. We leave it to the reader's own speculations as to what those conditions might be.

What options are now open to Terry, and could she have prevented this impasse without compromising her integrity? Again, we can only speculate. In challenging the school district's authority structure, Terry chose a rebellious strategy. This clashed with the administration's demand for conformity more typical of her colleagues. But rebellion works only if the individual has an effective power base both outside and within the organization. While the ACLU provided some support, there was no indication that Terry was trying to mobilize the support of her colleagues (perhaps by filing a grievance through the teacher organization, or through informal channels).

But other courses of action are also open to her. She could leave and go to a less conservative community where perhaps she would be more appreciated and ultimately more effective. As another alternative, before she was fired she could have chosen to "lay low" for awhile, appearing to go along, i.e., conform ritualistically, until the climate of opinion had changed. Meanwhile she might have worked quietly trying to build a base of support in the community, by working on behalf of influential groups hoping to gain their support. Perhaps she could try waiting to reinstate her actions until the administration became embroiled in another issue, and hence in a weaker position.

As still another alternative, she might have tried to innovate, that is, find a way to implement her principles without the bad publicity that had upset the administration. She might have somehow turned her liberal zeal to causes that are supported by the school district. Or, she could have suggested a meeting with representatives of the administration, parents and other community groups. Each side could present its views, explain the benefits and costs of Terry's actions from its own point of view, and prepare each other for ways of coping with problems and suggesting compromises. In such a meeting, Terry might suggest to parents ways in which they could constructively prepare their children for the controversial book, and the administration could be sure Terry understood how possible repercussions on the budget could affect her colleagues or other programs. We leave other possibilities to the reader's imagination.

In drawing conclusions, we must remember that this is a publicly controlled service organization subject to local political and legislative processes. The issue raised here might have developed in very different directions in a military organization, a business, or a church, where different controls and values are operating.

Activity 4—
*Bridge on the River Kwai**

Bridge on the River Kwai is one feature length film that is likely to stimulate enthusiastic discussion. Participants view the film (or read the novel) and examine the organizational characteristics and behaviors of three armies—British, Japanese, and American—each of which is involved in the building of a bridge across the Kwai River.

Some proposals for the use of the film and a set of discussion questions are suggested below. They are followed by a film review and analysis.

The film review and analysis might help prepare the instructor for introducing the film and for facilitating discussion at its conclusion.

It is suggested that the discussion questions be distributed to participants before they view the film. Some questions are suggested below:

- What are the main characteristics of each military organization?
- Which organizational characteristics contribute to the effective operation of the British army?
- What contrasts do you see in the organization of the British, Japanese, and American armies?
- What is the significance of the bridge building to the British and Japanese armies (as organizations)?
- How did technical competence influence the balance of power and authority?

At the conclusion of the film, participants may choose to discuss the film, write an analysis, or both. Everyone will have insights into the film, and perhaps the analysis should begin with a description of the military organization and its basic characteristics. Once basic concepts are understood, participants may choose their questions or address the questions provided.

MAJOR CONCEPTS

- Social system
    deliberateness
    permanence
    complexity
- Formal organization
- Bureaucracy

---

*Film can be rented through a Columbia Pictures distributor for approximately $50 per day. The novel by Pierre Boulle is published by Time, Inc. and Vanguard Press. There are many films, television programs, and novels depicting organizational problems which can be profitably analyzed as a way of enriching and testing one's knowledge. (See the suggested film list in Appendix B.)

- Delegation
- Slippage
- Standardization
- Supervision
- Power and authority
- Individual vs. organization needs
- Intraorganizational goal conflict
- Rational model for studying organizations

MAJOR FILM CHARACTERS

- Colonel Nicholson—commander of the British troops
- Colonel Saito—Japanese prison camp commander
- Major Clipton—British army medical officer
- Major Hughes—British officer and former mining company director
- Captain Reeves—British officer and former public works engineer
- Colonel Green—British officer in Calcutta in charge of clandestine services
- Major Shears (book only)—British officer in charge of blowing up the bridge
- Shears (film only)—American soldier and Japanese prisoner-of-war, member of the team assigned to blow up the bridge
- Captain Warden—British officer and language specialist assigned to blow up the bridge
- Lieutenant Joyce—demolition specialist and youngest member of the team assigned to blow up the bridge

THE FILM IN BRIEF

The film opens as the British Colonel Nicholson and the battered remainder of his batallion march in formation into a Japanese prison camp in Malaya during World War II. From the outset Colonel Nicholson and Colonel Saito, the prison camp commander, are locked in a confrontation based on personal and national pride, rank and authority.

Colonel Saito has been charged with the task of building a bridge across the Kwai River which will be the major link in the Burma-Siam railway. To carry out the task he needs the manpower of the British prisoners-of-war, but Colonel Nicholson refuses to permit his troops to take orders from the Japanese. He cites the Hague Convention and will not allow the Japanese to employ British officers as laborers. In the contest of wills that ensues, Colonel Nichonson is brutally tortured. He endures the savage treatment and proves to the Japanese that only by permitting British officers to plan and execute the construction project will the almost impossible job be completed on time. Colonel Saito must swallow his pride and sacrifice his authority to Nicholson. To Shears, the only American soldier in the camp, the two colonels are absurd.

As the bridge begins to rise, it becomes a symbol to Colonel Nicholson of his own professional pride and of the pride of the British Empire. While he drives his men relentlessly to prove their superiority to the Japanese, a British army unit in Calcutta is planning to destroy the bridge. Shears, having escaped from prison camp, becomes part of the demolition team. Their plans to wreck the bridge are finalized just as the bridge nears completion.

One evening as Colonel Nicholson proudly surveys his achievement, Colonel Saito observes the scene beaten and humiliated. Having lost in the ludicrous conflict of wills, he knows he has no choice but to take his own life.

Shortly thereafter the demolition team proceeds undercover to the edge of the Kwai and rigs the bridge with explosives. Colonel Nicholson, watching his troops march over the bridge and out of sight, spots the explosive cables exposed in the sand and tries desperately to save the bridge from destruction. Shears, observing from nearby, scrambles to rescue the detonator from Colonel Nicholson. Both are killed as the bridge collapses into the Kwai.

BRIDGE ON THE RIVER KWAI—A FILM ANALYSIS

The **Bridge on the River Kwai** provides an opportunity for sharpening the participant's understanding of organization theory. It contains clear examples of some characteristics of an organization and of the behavior of people operating within the organization's structure. Any number of questions may be raised or conclusions drawn while viewing this film. The discussion that follows will highlight some of the concepts a student is likely to identify as significant.

Testing Basic Concepts

Before proceeding to an analysis and debate, it is important to identify the basic elements of organization illustrated in the film.

First, the prison camp is a **social system.** It uses and processes materials, personnel, and information in order to turn out productive prisoners of war. The prison camp has been deliberately established by the Japanese; it has some degree of permanence and will last at least as long as the war; it is a complex set of interrelationships among people, rules, and the structure of the system.

Second, the prison camp is a **formal organization** made up of subgroups and members sharing a collective identity and performing certain activities. Within the prison camp three other formal organizations are also represented: the Japanese army, the British army, and the American army as seen through Shears. Each of these armies is a deliberately created, permanent, and complex social system. Each consists of subgroups (officers, combat units, medical unit, etc.) and has an authority structure, a collective identity, a division of labor, a roster of members, a program of activity, and procedures for replacing members.

Third, each of the military organizations is a particular type of formal organization termed **bureaucracy.** In the film, the bureaucratic characteristics of the British and Japanese armies are especially evident. The bureaucracy is based on a system of graded levels of authority and on strict compliance of subordinates with the commands of their superiors. Colonels Saito and Nicholson have been appointed to their positions on the basis of their expertise, have life-term tenures, and administer their organizations according to strict rules and regulations. Under their commands, the labor is divided into special jurisdictions of activity to carry out the tasks they assign.

However, some principles of bureaucracy are violated. For example, the individual personality and personal needs of the employees interfere with their professional roles and demands of their positions. It would be impossible to understand the events in **Bridge on the River Kwai** without knowledge of the personal characteristics of Saito, Shears, Nicholson, and others. Through understanding them as individuals, their actions make more sense.

Moreover, there are some important differences in the way the three bureaucracies operate. British soldiers seem anxious to give their unquestioning obedience to their commander, accepting both his goals and his means as their own. They are less willing than the U.S. soldier to use their own discretion. Nicholson then cements their loyalty by refusing publicly to relinquish command to the Japanese. Their loyalties to him, and to each other, are reinforced by their mutual hatred of the enemy as he endures torture to protect the organization's autonomy.

Central Themes

Several themes run through this case. In the first instance, Colonel Nicholson and Colonel Saito are pitted against one another in a struggle for power and authority. Colonel Saito, in his position as commander of the prison camp, assumes he has absolute authority to direct the actions of his men and the prisoners. He is challenged by Colonel Nicholson, who, in citing the Hague Convention and in demonstrating his ability to control his men, proves he has not only the authority but the power to command his troops. Although tortured, he persists in the struggle to wrest power from Colonel Saito and eventually the Japanese Colonel must yield to Nicholson if the objective of building the bridge is to be met. When the British demonstrate their technical expertise to be far superior to the Japanese, Colonel Nicholson gains the power and authority necessary to command both British and Japanese troops. Colonel Saito is humiliated as an individual even though his military objectives have been advanced.

At stake here is a fundamental conflict between two bases of authority. The Japanese commander's power and authority rest on his rank as the camp commander. But because he needs the British manpower and technical skills, he is forced to bargain with the British officer. Nicholson's technical expertise and the loyalty of his soldiers is his basis of power and authority, which he uses to gain the upper hand.

The second theme concerns tension between the individual and the organization to which he belongs. While Colonel Saito knows he must complete the bridge to meet the demands of the Japanese army, he also has a need to save face and to preserve his own integrity. When he must sacrifice his personal needs for the organization, he is destroyed and can be redeemed only by taking his own life.

Colonel Nicholson's objectives are also in opposition to those of the British army. To the British the bridge is a key to the strategic strength of the enemy and must be destroyed. To Nicholson it is a symbol of his prowess as a leader and of the superior status of the British army. It must be preserved as a monument to both. In his attempt to preserve that monument and to subvert the military objective of his own army, he is destroyed.

Another theme builds throughout the film as one group of British soldiers under Nicholson executes the building of the bridge, while a second unit, based in India, simultaneously is planning the destruction of the bridge. Obviously only one of the goals can be reached. The two British units confront one another on the Kwai River. Colonel Nicholson is killed and the bridge is destroyed.

Note that Nicholson seems to use two coping strategies at different stages of the drama. His first response is to rebel against the Japanese command. The Japanese respond by assimilating him into a leadership position, thus coopting him. He is now exerting his leadership on behalf of the Japanese interests. His second strategy comes under the heading of innovation. He accepts the enemies' goals while rejecting the means they originally proposed to relinquish his command. Instead, he is satisfied when he obtains control of the situation. The result can be called *goal displacement,* which is a term sometimes used when the original objective, in this case, victory, is replaced by what was formerly seen as a means to the end, i.e., the application of technical expertise to an engineering problem.

Models of Organization

The film also can be used to illustrate different models of organization, and to demonstrate the hazards sometimes involved in trying to apply models blindly to complicated situations.

In several respects the British and Japanese armies resemble *rational* organizations. Authority is based on expertise, control is centralized, the necessary information is available for making informed decisions, goals are clear-cut, and activities are well planned and closely coordinated. Saito's decision to defer to Nicholson's technical expertise was rational from the point of view of the organizational goals.

In most other respects the situation can be better understood by starting from the premises of the *organic* model. Neither Saito nor Nicholson was in full control, because one had rank in the camp but the other had the expertise. Consequently, power was split. Saito was forced to compromise with Nicholson who, in turn, achieved his position through a bargain with the Japanese. Colonel Nicholson's behavior makes no sense within the rational model, but it is an excellent illustration of how the specialized interests of a subgroup (his unit) can take precedence over the overall military goals of the British army. The status and achievements of his unit assumed priority for him out of all proportion to his organizational mission. How did this happen? The fact that the unit was insulated and isolated from the rest of the British army was an important factor. But the situation is not unique. Authority had been delegated to Nicholson by British commanders. There is always some tendency for slippage to occur as orders are passed down the hierarchy. The top officials were therefore forced to rely on Nicholson's discretion. They probably would not have been able to maintain complete control over him even under the best of circumstances.

Activity 5—
Vignettes
by Donald R. Cruickshank

Vignettes are short descriptions of situations that usually depict a single problem. But single problems are often influenced by a host of organizational rules, norms, and characteristics. The vignettes that follow were selected because they represent problems with which most teachers can identify. They also illustrate the kinds of problems participants can draw from their own experience. Therefore the instructor may use some or all of the vignettes and/or have participants write their own. Using a hypothetical problem initially may foster a measure of objectivity because participants are removed from the situation. However, it is even more instructive if participants report and discuss vignettes that they themselves have experienced to provide real application of awareness and knowledge of organization theory. From real situations participants can analyze the effectiveness of different approaches and share outcomes, continued analysis, and evaluation.

When participants have completed Part II, the group may wish to focus discussion on some of the specific concepts introduced in that section. The vignettes are concerned with schools and some organizational problems which emerge in the school setting. Each vignette deals primarily with one of the following concepts:

- Informal organization
- Organization models
- Teacher-colleague roles
- Status inconsistency

One or more of the vignettes may be used, in any order, during a discussion period. Participants should be provided with copies of the vignette and related discussion questions. Before the questions are considered it will be helpful to begin the discussion by defining and describing the problem as accurately as possible. The group may also identify the characteristics of the organization which may cause the problems to emerge.

TO TYPE OR NOT TO TYPE? THAT IS THE QUESTION

Concept: Informal Organization

Frequently other teachers ask students to do typing for them in typing class. Today, for example, one of my students brought in work from a teacher who is a good friend of mine. I hesitated, but finally agreed to let him do the typing, mainly on the basis of friendship. Before I knew it, the boy had distributed the material to be typed to three of his friends. When I intervened, the kids were very angry because they like the teacher too. My questions are:

- How can I maintain good relationships with students and fellow faculty members in this kind of situation?
- Are my class and my values about how it should be run more important than student and faculty rapport?
- Do I exclude office work too? The principal often sends in work when the school secretary is overloaded or absent.
- I am the PTA representative, and the PTA asks my students to do its work because it has no real secretary or office. What is a typing teacher to do?

OUR FACTORY (SCHOOL)

Concept: Organization Models

I'm not working in a factory, but all I hear lately from my principal is talk about the product (he means the students), accountability (he means whether the student is learning), and the instructional subsystem (he means the way I teach). The superintendent is on an efficiency kick and has mentally converted our school system into an industrial complex. We think we know what he is after, but why not use educational language? Some teachers are really turned off by this jargon. We all agree that kids are in school to learn and that we are there to help them. We all want to do that to the best of our ability. But that basic goal gets obscured and threatened when we are forced to write behavioral objectives, criterion-referenced tests, and so forth. These things just make teachers mad or at least annoyed. My questions are:

- Do superintendents and principals really believe that teachers don't want students to learn?

- Why do they have to use factory terminology when referring to our work in schools?
- How can we make them know that their purposes and goals do not come through clearly, and that the things they have us do seem to detract from the time we have to teach?
- Is there any evidence that writing behavioral objectives or criterion-referenced tests makes a teacher better? Better at what?

"MY BROTHER'S KEEPER?"

Concept: Teacher-Colleague Roles

Today I tried with great effort to maintain a professional attitude toward a fellow teacher who is older than I, whose discipline is terrible, whose tales should not be repeated, who drinks, and who is in general a very poor example for the students in her classes. For their sakes I wish that she would be a better person. She was very trying today with her talk about students and other teachers. My questions are:

- Should I ignore the tactics of a fellow teacher who is a harmful influence in the school?
- What is my role? Am I responsible to myself? The school staff? The community? My colleague?

RANK HAS ITS PRIVILEGE?

Concept: Status Inconsistency

Older teachers in our school have special privileges that I think are highly questionable. Many of them are certainly not the best teachers. They enjoy these privileges because of seniority. For example, they have first choice on parking spots, have the largest and best classrooms, have the most and newest equipment, influence the principal when students are assigned to teachers, receive more money, and so forth. I believe that teachers should get privileges and rank according to merit. Let the best teacher, not the oldest, have rewards. This way there would be incentives for doing the job. My questions are:

- How can teachers who are working hardest and contributing most get the rewards?
- How can teachers whom many of us consider almost senile be removed or at least not be rewarded?
- How can the school and community fairly determine who are the best teachers so that they can be rewarded?

Activity 6—
Up Against the Organization

Everyone has encountered a problem either caused or aggravated by an organization. When the individual attempts to resolve the problem through efforts to get the organization to change or to take action, the individual is often frustrated. However, if persistent, the person who understands organizations can often get the organization to move. One unfamiliar with organization behavior will often learn a great deal in the encounter.

The task for the participant during this activity is to select a past or current encounter he or she has experienced with an organization. Then, orally or in writing:

- Describe the problem
- Describe the steps taken to resolve the problem
- Describe how the organization responded
- Describe the outcome

When the description is complete, the participant will analyze what happened from an organization perspective. This may be done in writing or orally with the group's assistance.
Participants might select problems such as:

- Getting an incorrect bill acknowledged and altered by the company issuing the bill
- Getting a reserved parking place where "faculty only" or "officers only" or "car pools only" rules apply
- Attending a closed session of a meeting which you have a right to attend

During the analysis, they will consider questions such as:

- What characteristics of the organization may have created or aggravated the problem?
- What characteristics make it difficult for the organization to be responsive?
- What causes an organization to feel threatened?
- What causes an organization to respond to threats?
- What is necessary if the balance of power is to be shifted from the organization to the individual?
- What weapons does the organization use against the individual?

Postscript

In this volume, the first of a series, we have introduced rich and potentially useful literature on organizations. We have not tried to cover the topic thoroughly. Instead, we have sought to illustrate how a blend of materials—concepts, descriptions, case studies, films, and related exercises—can be used in conjunction, to illuminate perspectives on organizations. We have proceeded on the assumption that some basic knowledge about organization, together with some experience with analysis, will help people influence or cope with the circumstances in which they find themselves. The approach used here compliments the so-called organizational development (OD) approach. But it is not the same thing. Our approach relies less on developing a person's interpersonal skills and planning and administrative abilities, and relies more on enlarging one's understanding of social settings in which the person must function.

The target audience of this volume is also different. We have concentrated on developing the awareness and understanding of teachers, whereas such materials usually have been designed for administrators and other leaders. This new emphasis seems particularly relevant at a time when there is so much talk about participatory democracy and decentralizing decision making. Many observers who long for a more humane society pin their hopes on organizational reform. To some, this suggests a return to simpler ways, to smaller contexts, to former ways of doing things, even to less complex organizations. We doubt that this is possible. Our society is now too dependent on large, complex organizations. But people can learn to deal with big organizations in new ways that will give them more control over their destiny. The hope, then, is not in the past. It lies in cultivating the knowledge, attitudes, and skills which will enable people at all levels of complex organizations to deal more effectively with their problems. Such a goal is particularly appropriate for teachers. For although teachers work independently in isolated classrooms, they are part of one of the world's largest organizational networks—the American school system.

This volume will be followed by two others which will provide additional case materials and more detailed analyses of the school, community, and the state, all organizations about which teachers must become more knowledgeable.

Appendix A

Abstracts of Selected Readings

by Theodore C. Wagenaar

Becker, H. "Social Class Variations in the Teacher-Pupil Relationship." *Journal of Educational Sociology* 25 (1952): 451-65.

CONCEPTS: Lower-class students and their teachers

SUMMARY: Major problems of workers in service occupations are likely to arise from their relationship to their clients. Such workers often have some image of the ideal client. Teachers react differently to students of various social classes in terms of the problems of teaching, discipline, and moral acceptance.

Concerning the problem of teaching, teachers like to see progress; lower-class students seem to teachers to make progress more difficult. Many teachers include different teaching techniques for lower-class students, and principals have lower levels of expectations of these teachers. Discipline is a continual battle for teachers; teachers generally feel that lower-class students are more aggressive, less respectful, and more of a discipline problem. As a result, teachers of these students are more stern and employ physical punishment more often. Lower-class students are also less morally acceptable to teachers. Teachers view lower-class students as violating middle-class standards of cleanliness and health, sex and aggression, ambition and work. In short, teachers, who are generally middle class, view lower-class students as less morally acceptable and as posing more problems for teaching and discipline.

ABSTRACTOR'S NOTE: The author contends that as important socializers, teachers serve to reinforce the middle-class bias of schools. Lower-class students are repeatedly told they are inferior, and they begin to believe it (the Pygmalion effect). More teachers are needed who are less bound up in a definition of the ideal client. Compare this article to that of Sjoberg, Brymer, and Farris, which illustrates why lower-class clients have difficulty in dealing with service organizations.

This article is based on interviews with 60 teachers in Chicago in 1950.

Becker, H. "The Teacher in the Authority System of the Public School." *Journal of Educational Sociology* 27 (1953): 128-41.

CONCEPTS: Role of parents, teacher authority

SUMMARY: The role of the teacher in the school is considered vis-à-vis parent, principal, and colleagues. The teacher generally regards parental intrusion as a threat to his or her authority over students and over what is taught. The teacher is the professional, and sees the parent as someone who knows little about educational matters. Teachers particularly try to avoid confrontations with high-status parents. They use various coping mechanisms to deal with parents, such as referring parents to the principal.

The principal is accepted as the supreme authority in the school. Teachers generally expect the principal to back them up in disputes with parents. Principals are also expected to support teachers in dealing with students and to recognize the professional independence of teachers.

With regard to colleagues, teachers feel they should cooperate to defend themselves against attacks on their authority from parents and principals, and that they should refrain from directly endangering the authority of another teacher.

ABSTRACTOR'S NOTE: The author contends that outside the classroom, the authority position of teachers is somewhat limited; thus, other teachers and the principal are expected to support what authority teachers do have. Parents, who are external to the system of institutional control, are seen by teachers as a particular threat to their authority.

This article is based on interviews with 60 teachers in Chicago in 1950.

Bidwell, C. "The School as a Formal Organization." In J.G. March, ed., *The Handbook of Organizations.* Chicago: Rand McNally, 1965, pp. 972-1022.

CONCEPTS: School as bureaucracy, structural looseness
SUMMARY: Schools can be viewed as bureaucratic organizations:

1. They have a division of labor; that is, people do specific tasks for which they are trained.

2. These roles are organized into specific positions.

3. These positions are arranged hierarchically so that each person in a position is responsible to someone in a higher position.

4. Rules and specific procedures determine how schools are run.

School activities must be arranged in this organized fashion because schools are responsible for a uniform product of a certain quality and because socializing children for adult roles is a massive and complex task. But the problem of variability in student abilities demands a great deal of professional autonomy for teachers; teachers must be able to make situation-specific decisions in day-to-day teaching. Schools are not completely bureaucratic. Autonomy of teachers in the classroom and independence of schools from one another within a system result in structural looseless. Several characteristics of schools promote this structural looseness:

1. Teachers need professional autonomy to deal with individual student needs.

2. Because all students are compelled to attend school, the school must be flexible to deal with various student needs and interests.

3. Schools are responsible to the government and the public and must deal with the demands made; a highly bureaucratic form of organization would make adaptation difficult.

Clark, B.R. "Interorganizational Patterns in Education." In M.B. Brinkerhoff and P.R. Kuntz, eds., *Complex Organizations and Their Environments.* Dubuque, Iowa: Wm. C. Brown, 1972, pp. 356-66.

CONCEPTS: Organizational change, outside change
SUMMARY: Organizations respond to changes in the economic and political situation in two general ways: within the organization, and in response to outside demands. The inside approach involves changes suggested by organizational members; all decisions and actions involve only official members. The outside approach involves changes suggested and implemented by experts who are not official organizational members; such changes are often adopted on the basis of the expertness and legitimized role of the outsiders. The inside approach is often referred to as the organizational approach, whereas the outside approach is the interorganizational approach because the outsiders involved are often members of organizations other than the one being changed. The two approaches differ in that the interorganizational approach:

1. uses more personal, less formal procedures to deal with problems;

2. stresses teacher-to-teacher contact rather than teacher-to-administrator contact;

3. does not impose strictly defined standards of work;

4. employs more interpersonal, informal procedures to make decisions.

An example of the interorganizational approach is the reform of the science curriculum in the late 1950s by the Physical Science Study Committee (PSSC), a group of highly respected scientists.

Impetus developed from the Sputnik episode; America responded to this Russian accomplishment by attempting to improve science education. PSSC was independent and was funded by the National Science Foundation (NSF), an independent federal agency. Private foundations also provided support. Curriculum materials were marketed through commercial channels. Thus, PSSC became an important mechanism of national influence by doing research and development the textbook industry was not doing. NSF also initiated and supported a program of summer institutes through colleges; the program was very successful because directors of institutes at these colleges were looking for good materials. Local education authorities also participated in the implementation process. Participation was voluntary, but the quality of materials, respectability of the scientists, and the "bandwagon effect" led to immediate widespread adaptation of materials (50% of the nation's high school physics students were using the materials within six years). In sum, the process was set in motion from the top by an independent federal agency and was based on expertise; the process was broken down into specific tasks; the quality of the materials and the expertise of the sponsors sold the program more effectively than did administrative directives to adopt it. The whole process took place completely outside normal organizational channels, such as the state department of education.

Changing economic, political, and population conditions will make this type of response to the need for change more common.

Cole, S. *The Unionization of Teachers.* New York: Praeger, 1969.

CONCEPTS: Teacher militancy, teacher unionism

SUMMARY: There were four significant factors in the historical development of the United Federation of Teachers (1916-1968):

1. Teachers were intensely dissatisfied with salaries because of inflation and because salaries were already low in comparison to other professions.

2. They were dissatisfied with working conditions, such as over-crowded classrooms, discipline problems, and textbook shortages.

3. The civil rights movement of the 1960s made civil disobedience more acceptable to teachers.

4. Union leaders were developed and militancy was increasingly accepted by teachers.

Several other characteristics are associated with participation in teachers' unions:

1. Teachers who are Democrats are more militant because of their prolabor feelings.

2. Teachers who are Jews are more militant because of their prolabor sentiment and the fact that Jews are more committed to raising professional standards. This latter characteristic may be true primarily for the upwardly mobile New York City Jews studied by Cole.

3. Teachers of lower-class origins are more militant because of more contact with prolabor people. Their fathers are often union men.

4. Teachers who are males are more militant because they see their peers with the same level of education making more money, whereas females see their peers in lower-paid jobs or as housewives; also, men are usually the sole breadwinners and need a good salary whereas female teachers' income is often a second income.

5. Younger teachers are more militant because of their greater social liberalism; they have less to lose in terms of seniority; they are more likely to come from middle-class homes and therefore have less experience with the work ethic; and older teachers went to college during a time when the teacher was defined as a public servant who did not strike.

Elementary teachers are quite dissatisfied with working conditions, whereas secondary teachers are dissatisfied with the prestige of teaching as an occupation. The difference may be that secondary teachers are primarily males. Males are more likely than females to feel dissatisfied with the prestige of teaching when they compare their occupation to those of friends with similar levels of education.

Some teachers predisposed toward militancy (that is, Democrats, Jews, males, teachers of lower-

69

class origin, etc.) do not actually become militant. The extent to which a teacher's friends in the school supported the New York City strike was a significant factor in determing whether a teacher predisposed toward militancy actually became militant. Another contextual effect is the proportion of males on a staff; female teachers are considerably more militant if they are in a school with a high proportion of men. Still another effect is the presence of effective union leadership; this factor was most important where strike support was weakest, that is, in elementary schools.

Many teachers experienced cross pressures; that is, they had personal characteristics predisposing them toward militancy, but taught in schools where most of their friends did not support the New York City strike. They also experienced cross pressures when friends split between supporting the strike or not. Teachers often responded with avoidance behavior—calling in sick instead of deciding whether to strike or not. In fact, the more cross pressures teachers experienced, the more avoidance behavior was employed. Also, the more fear expressed by teachers, the more they engaged in avoidance behavior. But, if support for the strike among friends existed, fear was more easily overcome.

ABSTRACTOR'S NOTE: The author makes the following significant points: (a) teacher militancy is not a recent phenomenon; (b) several personal characteristics of teachers are associated with militancy; and (c) reference groups of teachers—people teachers regard as important—are significant factors in determining whether teachers predisposed toward militancy actually become militant.

Corwin, R.G. "The New Teaching Profession." In K. Ryan, ed., *Teacher Education.* 74th Yearbook of the National Society for the Study of Education, Part II. Chicago: University of Chicago Press, 1975, pp. 230-64.

CONCEPTS: Teacher militancy
SUMMARY: Teacher militancy can take many forms, including work stoppages, collective bargaining, and political action.

Work stoppages among teachers date back to 1918, but the prevalence, scope, strength, and defiance of teacher strikes are new. By 1968, 10% of the nation's teaching force was on picket lines.

The National Education Association (NEA) has played an increasingly important role in teacher militancy. The NEA, representing well over half of the nation's two million teachers, was not involved in a single work stoppage between 1952 and 1963, but participated in one-third of the 1966 work stoppages; 80% of the striking teachers that year were NEA members. The NEA and its affiliates have initiated 70% of the 720 work stoppages, strikes, and interruptions of service since 1960. The percentage of teachers who believe that it is right for teachers to strike has correspondingly risen sharply in recent years. Whereas only one out of two teachers surveyed by the NEA in 1965 supported the right to strike, by 1970 nine out of 10 teachers supported some type of group action, and three out of four believed that at least in some circumstances, teachers should strike. Because of its broad membership base, the NEA is well equipped to deal with state and national levels, where the major issues are increasingly being decided.

In the area of collective bargaining, the number of school systems reporting teacher agreements increased 70% in the period of 1966-68, and there was a doubling of the number of systems that had experienced negotiations at least once. By 1970, more than half the nations's teachers had some form of written agreement. This legislative activity has provided legal support for militant activity.

Teacher organizations are also turning to political forms of action; over half the NEA's state affiliates have political action arms. Teachers are increasingly becoming involved in political affairs.

The issues involved in militancy generally revolve around the following: (a) salaries, a primary issue; (b) working conditions, such as reduction of the school year, duty-free lunch periods, and extra compensation for overtime; and (c) policy issues, such as representation in groups that determine curriculum policy and select materials.

Several explanations of teacher militancy can be offered:

1. Status deprivation of the occupation—teaching has not kept pace in terms of status and income with other occupations. However, there is evidence that the prestige of teaching has been increasing.

2. Social mobility—individuals who seek to improve their prestige, or new people coming into the profession, rebel against the limited opportunities for advancement in teaching and become militantly involved to advance the entire occupation.

3. Professionalization—teachers are becoming better educated, increasingly specialized, and more highly committed to their careers. Teachers have developed professional conceptions of their roles that sometimes conflict with aspects of the school bureaucracy.

4. Organizational power—competition between the American Federation of Teachers and the NEA, both of which are becoming increasingly powerful.

Potential consequences include:

1. Increased organized strength of teachers;

2. A shift in power and authority from superintendents, school boards, and principals to teachers and teacher organizations;

3. Alterations in administrative authority structures, that is, the development of dual authority structures comprising teachers and administrators;

4. A reduced capacity for innovation, decision making centralized at the state level may result in difficulties for local schools to depart from standard practices and conditions on which uniform salaries are based (see Iannaccone's paper—Bibliog. IV);

5. Public resistance to the demands of teachers which generally mean higher taxes.

ABSTRACTOR'S NOTE: Teacher militancy is a complex phenomenon. It invokes subtle uses of influence and political action as well as the direct application of power. And it must be understood within a larger context—the increased formal education and job specialization of teachers and the growing prestige of teaching as well as the fact that new types of people are entering the profession.

Militancy is a response to the frustration that members of an occupation experience when they see the occupation improving, but not in comparison to the gains made by other occupations.

Militancy involves (a) social forces operating within the occupation and the society, (b) organizational characteristics of schools, and (c) personal characteristics of teachers. The net result is and will be more authority for teachers.

Gross, N., J. Giaquinta, and M. Bernstein. *Implementing Organizational Innovations.* New York: Basic Books, 1971.

CONCEPTS: Organizational change, organizational innovation

SUMMARY: Change that was extensively studied in one elementary school involved transforming the teacher's role from traditional to catalytic; that is, from teacher as authoritarian lecturer to teacher as instructional aide.

Previous literature on change in organizations can be summarized as follows:

1. It focuses on changes that were suggested, but not necessarily implemented.

2. It emphasizes the rather doubtful impact of a change agent.

3. It focuses on innovation among individuals, not on organizational innovation.

4. It has many methodological problems.

5. It ignores the perspective of teachers.

6. It employs questionable indicators of implementation.

7. It focuses on overcoming initial resistance of organizational members.

Organizational innovation is distinguishable from organizational change. The latter involves change by members in terms of their role performance in the authority structure whereas innovation involves behavioral changes designed to solve specific problems.

Several antecedent conditions must exist for effective implementation of organizational innovation: external pressure, internal tension, a previous atmosphere of change, and an outside expert with a positive image.

Several attendant conditions are also important: clarity of the innovation, capability of members to innovate, necessary materials, compatibility of organizational arrangements with the innovation, and willingness of the staff to innovate. Absence of any one of these attendant conditions may explain why an innovation failed.

The main reason for failure of the innovation in the particular elementary school under study was that the administration failed to take account of the difficulties involved and did not provide feedback mechanisms.

ABSTRACTOR'S NOTE: This case study makes the following significant points: (a) organizational innovation is not a single event, but the result of a complex set of forces; (b) the role of the administration is crucial; and (c) organization members may have to be resocialized to a new frame of reference for effective innovation.

Herriott, R.E., and B.J. Hodgkins. "The Environment of American Educational Systems." In *The Environment of Schooling: Formal Education as an Open Social System.* Englewood Cliffs, N.J.: Prentice-Hall, 1973, pp. 32-60.

CONCEPTS: Education vs. community, regional, and social class differences; environment and school

SUMMARY: Contextual differences in education can be examined in terms of regional, community, and neighborhood differences.

Regional Differences. Modernity is defined as the extent to which a society or region "is characterized by a general acceptance and use of the most advanced available technological knowledge." American society can be divided into more-modern regions (Northeast, West, and Great Lakes) and less-modern regions (Plains and Southeast). The more-modern regions emphasize the following: individuality; progress, social morality (a social ethic oriented toward helping others); and material reward. Education in more-modern regions: (a) emphasizes skills and orientations necessary to contribute to the larger society; (b) is more specialized; (c) emphasizes tangible indicators of prestige, such as the proportion of students going on to college; (d) emphasizes adaptability to societal demands; (e) is more independent of the local social context; and (f) has more inputs, primarily expenditures.

Community Differences. Communities can be differentiated primarily in terms of rural versus urban. Rural communities (a) have small populations and low population densities; (b) are removed from urban areas; (c) stress agricultural occupations; (d) have a high level of community identification and solidarity; (e) are characterized by uniform ideologies and values; (f) have low levels of division of labor; (g) emphasize personal relationships; and (h) stress the importance of family.

Urban communities have characteristics opposite of rural. In terms of education, rural communities: reemphasize community solidarity and continuity, stress community requirements at the expense of school efficiency and effectiveness, and they are very sensitive to community feedback. Also, they are less specialized, have lower student-teacher ratios, and have fewer kindergartens and adult education programs. Further, they have older teachers, who teach several different subject areas or grades; have fewer teachers with college degrees; have higher levels of retardation and higher dropout rates; and place less emphasis on college attendance. Urban communities emphasize characteristics opposite of these.

Neighborhood Differences. Neighborhoods can be differentiated primarily in terms of social class. Middle-class persons stress equalitarian parental roles, have more permissive attitudes toward children, place high value on social activity, and tend to be associated with modern Protestant or Catholic churches. They emphasize work, achievement, rationality, and individuality; are optimistic and positive in their attitudes toward life; and stress opportunity. Lower-class persons stress opposite values. In terms of education, middle-class persons stress education in preparing students for adult roles; are better equipped to deal with large-scale organizations like the school (see Sjoberg, Brymer, and Farris); stress and attain achievement; and stress early participation in social, athletic, and community organizations to prepare children to deal with the school. Also, they stress rationality and individuality; stress role expectations congruent with school demands; have less retardation and lower dropout rates; attend schools that are predominantly middle class, and thereby experience a positive climate for achievement; and have better teachers and principals.

ABSTRACTOR'S NOTE: Because American society and schools are generally modern and middle-class-oriented, lower-class students have great difficulty coping and achieving. We should examine whether schools must be middle class and if so, how lower social-class parents can socialize their children with appropriate values.

Herriott, R.E., and B.J. Hodgkins. "American Public Education as an Open Socio-cultural System." In *The Environment of Schooling: Formal Education as an Open Social System*. Englewood Cliffs, N.J.: Prentice-Hall, 1973, pp. 67-104.

CONCEPTS: Open systems theory

SUMMARY: Social reality, and therefore life in organizations, can be analyzed from the perspective of open systems theory. The two fundamental concepts in this approach are *system* and *environment*. System can be defined as "a set of complex relationships evidencing a high degree of stability." A system is more than the sum of its parts; it is qualitatively different from the individual qualities of the parts. Environment can be defined as "those objects and patterns of relationships that exist outside a system but significantly influence it or are influenced by it." The boundaries between a system and its environment are not always clear and are constantly changing. *Energy* is "that which is exchanged between a system and its environment." Open systems exchange energy with their environments.

Key characteristics of open social systems include:

1. *Input*—the energy received by a system from its environment to help sustain it. Input is primarily in the form of information, materials, and personnel. Teachers, administrators, curriculum materials, and community values are input for the school.

2. *Throughput*—the focus of energy by the system. For the school the throughput is students.

3. *Output*—the energy expended by a system in performing its role. An example for the school is changes in students (knowledge).

4. *Negative entropy*—refers to the reduction of energy to a point at which no energy exists. Negative entropy exists when a system continually obtains new energy from the environment, thereby insuring a continued existence. Continued funding and a continued source of clientele are examples of negative entropy for the school.

5. *Feedback*—information that a system receives from the environment that helps it perform its purpose more effectively. Examples of feedback for the school are analysis of the academic performance of a school's graduates and feedback from influential people in the community.

6. *Homeostasis*—the steady state attained by systems, by continually regulating inputs and internal system happenings. Homeostasis requires balancing demands from various groups for school change.

7. *Structural differentiation*—As a result of continually obtaining new energy from the environment, the structure of a system tends to become more complex. For example, as schools serve wider areas with a diversity of student needs and characteristics, the structure of a school tends to become more complex and specialized.

Katz, F.G. "The School as a Complex Social Organization." *Harvard Educational Review* 34 (1964): 428-55.

CONCEPTS: Teacher autonomy

SUMMARY: Provisions for autonomy exist in most organizations, particularly schools. There are two ways of viewing organizations that have implications for autonomy. The most common way stresses the organization as a collection of individuals in pursuit of central goals; a second stresses the diversity of individual needs and problems in an organization. This second approach is more appropriate for schools because there are many different types of teachers and students, and teachers must have autonomy to deal with individual differences. Autonomy is defined as behavior not controlled by someone else; thus, separate subparts in an organization have some autonomy from each other and from the organization as a whole.

Autonomy of teachers has two bases—teacher specialization and the relationships that teachers develop within and outside the organization. The first basis reflects the autonomy that teachers need to meet individual student problems with their specialized knowledge. This basis of autonomy often conflicts with an administrative emphasis on strict control to insure uniform, calculable performance.

The second basis refers to relationships that teachers have with other people and groups within and outside the school. The more relationships the teacher has, the more autonomous the teacher generally is. Thus, teachers gain autonomy vis-à-vis the administration by actively participating in professional organizations. Such participation yields security and a source of power independent of the administration. The result is an unofficial license developed within a legitimate mode of organization. Autonomy gained in this manner often leads to conflicting loyalties because of responsibilities of involvement with both the administration and external organizations. The teacher can also develop autonomy by displaying strong commitment to the administration.

Characteristics of students also introduce autonomy provisions. The school exists in relation to family, peer groups, and occupational groups, and must have some autonomy from these agencies while simultaneously working with them. Because the student is a minor, legal provisions exist to guarantee student autonomy (for example, the recent Supreme Court decision asserting rights of suspended students). Students also develop autonomy via subcultures, the goals of which often conflict with basic school goals.

Kerr, N.D. "The School Board as an Agency of Legitimation." In S.D. Sieber and D.E. Wilder, eds., *The School in Society: Studies in the Sociology of Education.* New York: Free Press, 1973, pp. 380-400.

CONCEPTS: Role of school board

SUMMARY: There are three main forces shaping school board members' attitudes and performance: school board politics; socialization and pressures for conformity; and community pressures.

School Board Politics. School board members do not represent visible constituencies that support their election and monitor their performance. As a result, there are few issues involved in school board elections. Thus, new members are allowed freedom to adjust to the expectations of administrators and senior board members. Constituencies do not exist because members are uniformly upper class and do not represent issues differentially important to the various social classes. Similarly, the wide variety of parental interest blocks the emergence of clear issues regarding the school program.

New members are unfamiliar with school board activities and the school program. Regarding board activities, candidates do not realize the importance of behind-the-scenes decisions. Regarding the program, candidates display ignorance of programs already in operation and focus their attention on such noneducational issues as improving bus transportation and setting up citizen advisory groups.

Socialization and Pressures for Conformity. New members are carefully oriented to their new roles. The superintendent often invites new board members to an orientation in the superintendent's office before the first meeting. The member is given a great deal of information and told to direct problems to the superintendent. Senior board members make clear their expectations that the new member will be a learner and not a spokesperson. Condescension, paternalism, chiding, and humiliation occur often. Each new member is placed on a different committee to insure proper socialization. The ignorance of new members is used by older members to minimize their contributions. Above all, new members are taught that educational matters are the sole province of the superintendent and staff. Thus, most members' time is spend on financial matters and other noneducational issues.

Community Pressures. Many of the complex issues faced by the board are incompletely understood by the public. Public concern over such issues as whether one- or two-story school buildings were better and whether home economics should be taught (even though the state required it) made board members increasingly cynical about the value of representing the public. Member alienation from the public often results from the members' greater understanding of the needs of the system combined with the community's unwillingness to grant them superior knowledge. As a result, board members often conceal their activities from the public and present an appearance of unanimity.

ABSTRACTOR'S NOTE: As a result of these factors, school boards serve more to legitimize policies of the school system to the community than to represent various segments of the community.

Lortie, D. "The Balance of Control and Autonomy in Elementary School Teaching." In A. Etzioni, ed., *The Semi-Professions and Their Organization: Teachers, Nurses, Social Workers.* New York: Free Press, 1969, pp. 1-53.

CONCEPTS: School organization, teacher autonomy, teaching profession

SUMMARY: The unique position of the elementary school teacher is related to the relatively low level of professionalization and the high level of classroom autonomy. Reasons for the low level of professionalization include:

1. A history of lay control led to little importance attached to teaching, and to teachers defined more as employees than as professionals. Why have teachers not struggled to attain more complete professional standing?

2. There is little concern for clearly establishing criteria for membership in the profession. For example, are principals to be included?

3. Limited prestige and income are also functions of historical trends.

4. The feminization of the occupation historically meant low prestige and income because female teachers typically had a lower level of commitment and females were generally considered second class in the professions.

5. They lack a favored position in the market. Teachers cannot assert themselves without serious economic risk.

6. Teacher knowledge and skills are not recognized as vital to individual and social welfare, or as technical and specialized in nature.

7. States are willing to bypass licensing procedures for teachers, but not for doctors.

8. Self-governance among teachers is minimal.

9. The period of training to learn technical and moral practices is minimal compared to doctors.

10. The training offered to teachers is ill-understood and limited in usefulness.

The high level of classroom autonomy is due in large part to certain characteristics that differentiate the school from other organizations:

1. The school is a less well-developed organization:
   a. Boards of education do not have many significant powers.
   b. Few offices with power exist besides that of superintendent.
   c. Little agreement exists on which goals are most important and how to measure them.
   d. School systems do not have a detailed outline of policy (this point reinforces Bidwell's notion of structural looseness.
   e. Schools have certain characteristics that lessen the range and depth of administrative control.
   f. Schools have few avenues for promotion; that is, few formal ranks exist between teacher and principal. This feature further reduces control over teachers because they cannot be rewarded with a promotion.

g. Allocation decisions over budget, personnel, and students occur infrequently as compared to other organizations, which make such decisions frequently to adapt to changing needs.

2. It is more difficult to separate teachers' tasks than, for example, the tasks involved in the production of an automobile, which also makes control more difficult.

3. Little agreement exists on the best ways of teaching; thus, superiors cannot use specialized knowledge to control teachers, but must rely on their position of authority.

4. Because there is little agreement on teaching technique, schools are less rule oriented than other organizations.

Because the school has a weak control structure, the board is not able to control closely what goes on in the classroom, and, as a result, teachers have a high level of classroom autonomy. The board's lack of control over the classroom also means that boards have less control over demands by external agents such as pressure groups, and they are less able to resist the nationalizing trends in American education (mentioned by Wayland).

The reward structure of the school organization also has implications for classroom autonomy. Rewards are primarily intrinsic, that is, related to personal satisfactions derived from in-class teaching, rather than extrinsic (monetary). Because all teachers receive the same monetary rewards for a given level of experience and training, teachers who work more diligently do not necessarily receive greater monetary rewards. Thus, teachers strive to maximize their intrinsic, classroom-generated rewards and become more student oriented, less administration oriented. As a result, teachers become indifferent to the impact of organizational affairs on their relationships with the administration and colleagues, provided that their classroom autonomy is not violated. Teachers do resist manipulation of extrinsic, monetary rewards that would reduce this classroom autonomy (for example, merit pay and differentiated staffing).

ABSTRACTOR'S NOTE: Autonomy is a relative term; absolute autonomy would not be desirable. Autonomy is not synonymous with power, the ability to impose one's will on another, which teachers do not possess. Autonomy is not synonymous with authority, legitimized power, which teachers also lack. Autonomy and control are independent dimensions, not opposite ends of one continuum.

Perrow, C. "Why Bureaucracy?" In *Complex Organizations: A Critical Essay*. Glenview, Ill.: Scott, Foresman, 1972, pp. 1-60.

CONCEPTS: Bureaucracy, complex organization

SUMMARY: Basically an organization: (a) should be conducted on a continual basis; (b) has a hierarchy of offices, each office under control of a higher one; (c) contains people doing specific jobs for which they are trained; (d) should clearly define each person's role, responsibilities, and power; and (e) should have written rules to govern performance of duties.

Concerning rewards individuals should: (a) receive fixed salaries, graded by rank; (b) not own the means of production; (c) separate their private affairs and property from that of the organization; (d) account for their use of organizational property; and (e) make their office/position their primary occupation.

The individuals themselves: (a) serve voluntarily and are appointed; (b) their service constitutes a career, with promotions according to seniority or achievement; (c) they owe allegiance to the position that someone occupies, not to the individual filling that position; (d) they are subject to authority only with respect to their official obligations; and (e) they have the right to appeal decisions and to state their grievances.

Complete bureaucracy is never realized because:

1. Unwanted extraorganizational influences on the behavior of members cannot be eliminated.

2. An organization cannot adequately adapt to demands for rapid change.

3. People are only average in intelligence, etc.

Common criticisms of bureaucracy are: it is inflexible, inefficient, and it stifles the spontaneity, freedom, and self-realization of employees. On the other hand, "bureaucracy is a form of organization superior to all other (forms of organization) we know or can hope to afford in the near and middle future." Examples of beneficial features of bureaucratic characteristics are:

1. Greater effectiveness results from using universalistic procedures, where everyone gets the same treatment, instead of particularistic procedures where friends and relatives get special treatment.

2. Tenure rewards people for going through a long period of formal training.

3. Separating organizational and private affairs results in less appropriation of organizational property for private use, and higher overall effectiveness.

4. Rules are needed when complexity increases so that an organization can operate effectively. Rules stem from past adjustments and help stabilize the present and future. Rules are often made the scapegoats for underlying problems, such as the premises on which an organization operates.

5. A hierarchy assists in reducing confusion because people know whom to consult about a problem. It also results in proper transmission of knowledge and commands.

The problem does not lie in any single component of bureaucracy. It lies in who controls the immense power that a bureaucracy generates and for what purposes or goals this power is applied.

ABSTRACTOR'S NOTE: Perrow's chapter is a lucid analysis of the basic characteristics of bureaucratic organizations. Perrow stresses the positive aspects of bureaucracies. He suggests that rather than examining the organizational characteristics, we look at both who controls organizations and what goals are followed, to get at the source of many problems ascribed to the bureaucracy.

Sjoberg, G., R. Brymer, and B. Farris. "Bureaucracy and the Lower Class."*Sociology and Social Research* 50 (1966): 325-37.

CONCEPTS: Bureaucracy, lower class

SUMMARY: Two main characteristics of the relationship between bureaucracies and lower-class clients serve to reinforce the culture of poverty. First, service organizations generally cannot and do not meet the needs of lower-class clients. Second, lower-class clients are inadequately prepared to cope with service organizations.

Features of service organizations that preclude efficient and effective service for lower-class clients are:

1. Staffing arrangements result in reduced quality of service (for example, the high proportion of first-year teachers).

2. Personnel prefer working with clients who make it easier to achieve measurable goals, that is, middle-class clients.

3. Clients are more often blamed for poor service than the organization is. For example, IQ tests, which stress middle-class values, are used to characterize lower-class students as less intelligent; the students are held responsible rather than the organization.

4. The emphasis given to rules and standards often results in inadequate attention to the multiple and varied needs of lower-class clients.

5. Staff members are inadequately socialized into the world view of lower-class clients.

6. Emphasis on stability and control often stifles grievances of lower-class clients.

Lower-class clients have difficulty coping with service organizations because:

1. They lack knowledge about the rules of the game, that is, how to manipulate bureaucracies to their advantage.

2. Their contacts with the organization are confined to the lower echelons; staff members at this level are the most constrained by rules and standards.

3. They are less able to deal with people on an impersonal basis.

ABSTRACTOR'S NOTE: Compare this article to Becker's 1952 article, which also illustrates how service organizations work against lower-class clients.

Smith, L.M., and P.M. Keith. *Anatomy of Educational Innovation: An Organizational Analysis of an Elementary School.* New York: Wiley, 1971.

CONCEPTS: Change approaches, innovation

SUMMARY: The developers of a new school emphasizing individualized instruction tried to meet three developmental challenges in setting up the school: They tried to select a social base, that is, they examined the community environment to discover its resources and power structure. They tried to develop a homogeneous staff via selective recruiting and sharing of experiences. They tried to formalize procedures, that is, routine supervision and reliance on rules.

A number of problems developed:

1. The conservative community exerted pressure that resulted in administrative change in the central office, which in turn resulted in the loss of an innovative principal.

2. The carefully outlined program led to a covering up of internal problems, such as staff conflict.

3. Establishing the innovative school led to a great demand on resources (time, energy, personnel, and materials), which also led to staff conflict.

4. The school was new and had to develop a tradition and an appropriate set of norms to help guide behavior.

5. Selection of inexperienced teachers resulted in a limited pool of teaching skills, inability to handle children, and unimaginative teaching.

6. The fact that teachers had to develop all curriculum materials led to time problems for the staff.

7. Because the school was new, many emergent problems had to be dealt with. Meeting these problems often resulted in having to deal with still more problems that were not anticipated in meeting the first set of problems.

8. The so-called advantages of the physical plant were not always realized; for example, moveable partitions weren't very moveable, the openness of the building led to privacy problems for the staff.

9. Coordination problems developed, particularly within and among the teams of teachers.

10. Teachers working in specialized areas heightened the coordination problems.

11. The plan for an "upside-down authority structure," that is, making students the ultimate authority, didn't work out.

12. The developers tried to change too many things in too short a time period.

One major result was massive uncertainty. Teachers were not sure what roles to fill or how to fill them, they were unsure of the authority structure, and they were unsure of how to deal with staff conflict and how to cope when things did not go as planned.

Two general ways to change an organization are: the *revolutionary* approach, which stresses changing many different parts of the organization as rapidly as possible and is characterized by high risk and potentially great rewards; and the *gradualist* approach, which stresses the changing of only a few segments of the organization at a time. These two approaches can be compared:

Revolutionary	*Gradualist*
1. large-scale change	1. change broken up into small steps
2. emphasis on total policy	2. emphasis on development of subunits
3. changes limited to a specified time period	3. changes allowed to stretch beyond a specified time period
4. focus on one main avenue for change	4. allowance for multiple paths to change
5. no allowance for accelerated change	5. allowance for accelerated change
6. little provision for "locking in" change	6. maximal provision for "locking in" change
7. little cushioning provisions for special problems.	7. many cushioning provisions for special problems.

The problem with the revolutionary approach is that, because an organization has many interrelated parts, the revolutionary approach, with its emphasis on rapid large-scale change, produces several undesirable and unanticipated results and requires large amounts of resources. It also results in the problem of uncertainty mentioned above. The gradualist approach solves many of these problems.

Wayland, S. "Structural Features of American Education as Basic Factors in Innovation." In M. Miles, ed., *Innovations in Education*. New York: Teachers College Press, 1964, pp. 587-613.

CONCEPTS: Innovation, nationalization

SUMMARY: There is evidence of a national system of education in America which has implications for innovation. The evidence is as follows:

1. National recruitment of teachers, that is, teachers trained in one state can often teach in others;
2. The successful movement of students from school to school;
3. The national market for instructional materials;
4. The national examination system, such as the National Merit Scholarship Program.

Additionally, there are certain structures supporting a national system *(ancillary structures):* national organizations for teachers and administrators; the lack of a direct formal relationship between teacher training institutions and schools; and accreditation associations.

This national system retards educational innovation by imposing standards that local education authorities do not wish to violate. It also reduces attention to the needs of the local school system. When innovations are proposed, too much attention is focused on the attributes of the innovation and too little on the structures of educational systems and individual schools. More attention should be given to the role of the ancillary structures noted above and their impact on innovation.

ABSTRACTOR'S NOTE: In spite of the popular notion of local, lay control, the author illustrates that there is a national system of education and that this system works against educational innovation. Contrast this piece with the Clark article which illustrates how innovation occurs in spite of this national system.

Wirt, F.M., and M.W. Kirst. "The Local Conversion Process: Boards and Subsystems." In *The Political Web of American Schools*. Boston: Little, Brown, 1972, pp. 78-95.

CONCEPTS: Power of school board and superintendent; role of community, school board, and superintendent

SUMMARY: Both school boards and school professionals, superintendents, have influence on local educational policy. School board members generally are: business people or professionals, male, wealthy, about 45-55 years old, Republican, and long-term community residents. About half the members serve for "self-oriented" reasons, and half have "community-oriented" motives. Conflict between board and community often results because board members, being of high socioeconomic status, are more liberal in terms of expenditures and academic policies than the lower status community at large. School board members generally do not play a decisive role in educational decision making because:

1. They hold demanding jobs, which limit the amount of time they can spend on school matters.
2. They do not use performance criteria and objective data to evaluate their superintendents and schools.
3. They do not run on a specific platform and thus do not have a specific mandate from the community to act in a particular way.

At present, boards serve primarily to mediate among various sources of pressure and leave important policy issues to the professional staff, "and even in mediating they may do little." As a result, "they legitimate proposals of the professional staff, making only marginal changes, rather than representing citizens." In fact, boards often spend 80 percent of their time on managerial details and fail to deal with policy issues.

The superintendent has a considerable amount of power because the job includes: control of the agenda for board meetings; determination of school system organization; definition of alternatives for the board; research production; specific policy recommendations; hiring, assignment, promotion, and determination of tenure; and control of a specialized staff. The job is a full-time one which requires a specialist in the field.

Perhaps most of the superintendent's power develops from control of information. However, serving at the pleasure of the board, a superintendent can be replaced if conflicts develop or if a new board is elected.

Historically, the community has not displayed much interest in the management of the schools. Research indicates that citizens know very little about the substance of education or major policy issues. Most often, the public is concerned only with minor details or emotional issues, such as dress codes, discipline, and sex education. Thus, the school board will spend much of its time on such issues. Similarly, community leaders express little interest in basic educational issues.

Community control and decentralization represent more recent community efforts to reduce board and superintendent powers and increase the community's power. Community control would create several local education agencies out of one central system and thereby result in several new community-based school boards of local members. Decentralization would occur within the existing administration and under the single, central school board. In effect, field administrators would gain power from central administrators. Both community control and decentralization involve several value conflicts, particularly between democratic control and professional autonomy. Also, community involvement would presumably make participation in the schools more meaningful and personal; it would increase the control that community members desire over their lives. There is some dispute over whether community involvement would increase or decrease segregation. In addition, problems exist in the definition of district boundaries and personnel selection procedures.

Appendix B

Suggested Film List

David and Lisa
Caine Mutiny
A Thousand Clowns
Casablanca
Kes
Twelve Angry Men
Stalag 17
Adam's Rib
Guilty by Reason of Race
Blackboard Jungle
The Pawnbroker
Mr. Smith Goes to Washington
How the West Was Won, Lost, and Why Man Creates
High School
Children Without
One Flew Over the Cuckoo's Nest

Bibliography

I. Social Systems Theory

A. General

Hall, R.H. "Introduction." In *Organizations: Structure and Process.* Englewood Cliffs, N.J.: Prentice-Hall, 1972, pp. 3-38. See especially the section on perspectives, pp. 14-34.

Katz, D., and Kahn, R.L. "Organizations and the System Concept." In M. Brinkerhoff and P. Kuntz, *Complex Organizations and Their Environments.* Dubuque, Iowa: William C. Brown, 1972, pp. 33-47.

B. Applied to Education

Goslin, D.A. "The School as a Social System." In *The School in Contemporary Society.* Chicago: Scott, Foresman, 1965, pp. 19-41.

Griffiths, D.E. "System Theory and School Districts." In P.C. Sexton, ed. *Readings on the School in Society.* Englewood Cliffs, N.J.: Prentice-Hall, 1967, pp. 175-87.

Herriott, R.E., and Hodgkins, B.J. "American Public Education as an Open Sociocultural System." In *The Environment of Schooling: Formal Education as an Open Social System.* Englewood Cliffs, N.J.: Prentice-Hall, 1973, pp. 67-104. See especially pp. 67-96.*

Waller, W. "The School as a Social Organism." In S.D. Sieber and D.E. Wilder, eds. *The School in Society: Studies in the Sociology of Education.* N.Y.: The Free Press, 1973, pp. 34-39.

II. Organizational Behavior

A. General

Bidwell, C. "The School as a Formal Organization." In J.G. March, ed. *The Handbook of Organizations.* Chicago: Rand McNally, 1965, pp. 972-1022.*

Blau, P.M., and Meyer, M.W. *Bureaucracy in Modern Society,* 2nd ed. New York: Random House, 1971.

Drabek, T.E., and Haas, J.E. *Understanding Complex Organizations.* Dubuque, Iowa: Wm. C. Brown, 1974.

Hall, R.H. "Types of Organizations." In *Organizations: Structure and Process.* Englewood Cliffs, N.J.: Prentice-Hall, 1972, pp. 39-78. See especially pp. 42-60.

Perrow, C. "Why Bureaucracy?" In *Complex Organizations: A Critical Essay.* Glenview, Ill.: Scott, Foresman, 1972, pp. 1-60.*

B. Individuals in Organizations

Argyris, C. "Individual Actualization in Complex Organizations." In F.D. Carver and T.J. Sergiovanni, *Organizations and Human Behavior: Focus on Schools.* N.Y.: McGraw Hill, 1969, pp. 189-90.

Cole, S. *The Unionization of Teachers.* New York: Praeger, 1969.*

Corwin, R.G. "Professional Persons in Public Organizations." In Carver and Sergiovanni, 1969, op. cit., pp. 212-27.

Goffman, E. "The Characteristics of Total Institutions." In A. Etzioni, ed. *The Semi-Professions and Their Organization: Teachers, Nurses, Social Workers.* New York, The Free Press, 1969, pp. 312-38.

Merton, R.K. "Bureaucratic Structure and Personality." In Etzioni, 1969, op. cit., pp. 47-58.

Abstracts of items followed by asterisks appear in Appendix A.

C. Organizational Problems

Barnard, C.I. "Functions and Pathology of Status Systems in Formal Organizations." In Carver and Sergiovanni, 1969, op. cit., pp. 51-62.

Bell, G.D. "Formality Versus Flexibility in Complex Organizations." In Carver and Sergiovanni, 1969, op. cit., pp. 71-81.

Corwin, R.G. "Patterns of Organizational Conflict." In K. Azumi and J. Hage, eds. *Organizational Systems: A Text-Reader in the Sociology of Organizations.* Lexington, Mass.: D.C. Heath, 1972, pp. 397-411.

Litwak, E. "Models of Bureaucracy Which Permit Conflict." In Carver and Sergiovanni, 1969, op. cit., pp. 82-90.

Thompson, V.A. "Hierarchy, Specialization, and Organizational Conflict." In Carver and Sergiovanni, 1969, op. cit., pp. 18-41.

III. The School as a Complex Organization

A. General

Corwin, R.G. *Reform and Organizational Survival: The Teacher Corps as an Instrument of Educational Change.* New York: Wiley-Interscience, 1973.

Corwin, R.G. "The School as an Organization." In Sieber and Wilder, 1973, op, cit., pp. 164-87.

Corwin, R.G. "Models of Educational Organizations." In F.N. Kerlinger and J.B. Carroll, eds. *Review of Research in Education,* Vol. 2, Itasca, Ill.: F.T. Peacock, 1974, pp. 247-95.

Katz, F.G. "The School as a Complex Social Organization." *Harvard Educational Review* 34 (1964): 428-55.*

B. Consequences of Organization

Abbott, M.G. "Hierarchical Impediments to Innovation in Educational Organizations." In Carver and Sergiovanni, 1969, op, cit., pp. 42-50.

Boyan, N.J. "The Emergent Role of the Teacher in the Authority Structure of the School." In Carver and Sergiovanni, 1969, op. cit., pp. 200-211.

Cicourel, A.V., and Kitsuse, J.I. "The School as a Mechanism of Social Differentiation." In Sieber and Wilder, 1973, op. cit., pp. 219-29.

Coleman, J.S. "The Adolescent Subculture and Academic Achievement." In Sieber and Wilder, 1973, op. cit., pp. 265-74.

Dreeben, R. "The Contribution of Schooling to the Learning of Social Norms." In Sieber and Wilder, 1973, op. cit., pp. 62-77.

Goodlad, J.I., Klein, M.F. and Associates. *Behind the Classroom Door.* Worthington, Ohio: Charles A. Jones, 1970.

Gross, N., Giaquinta, J., and Bernstein, M. *Implementing Organizational Innovations.* New York: Basic Books, 1971.*

Jackson, P. "Organizational Constraints in the Classroom." In Sieber and Wilder, 1973, op. cit., pp. 212-18.

McDill, E.L., Rigsby, L.C., and Meyers, E.D., Jr. "Educational Climates of High Schools: Their Effects and Sources." In Sieber and Wilder, 1973, op. cit., pp. 112-33.

Moeller, G.H., and Charters, W.W. "Relation of Bureaucratization to Sense of Power among Teachers." In Carver and Sergiovanni, 1969, op. cit., pp. 235-48.

Moeller, G.H. "Bureaucracy and Teachers' Sense of Power." In Sieber and Wilder, 1973, op. cit., pp. 119-211.

Smith, L.M., and Keith, P.M. *Anatomy of Educational Innovation: An Organizational Analysis of An Elementary School.* New York: Wiley, 1971.*

C. Teaching as an Occupation

Becker, H. "Social Class Variations in the Teacher-Pupil Relationship." *Journal of Educational Sociology* 25 (1952): 451-65.*

Becker. H. "The Teacher in the Authority System of the Public School." *Journal of Educational Sociology* 27 (1953): 128-41.

Brenton, M. "Teachers' Organizations: The New Militancy." In L.M. Useem and E.L. Useem, eds. *The Education Establishment.* Englewood Cliffs, N.J.: Prentice-Hall, 1974, pp. 60-68.

Corwin, R.G. "The New Teaching Profession." In K. Ryan, ed. *Teacher Education. 74th Yearbook of the National Society for the Study of Education, Part II.* Chicago: University of Chicago Press, 1975, pp. 230-64.*

Gracey, H.L. *Curriculum or Craftsmanship: Elementary School Teachers in a Bureaucratic System.* Chicago: University of Chicago Press, 1972.

Lortie, D. "The Balance of Control and Autonomy in Elementary School Teaching." In A. Etzioni, ed., op. cit., pp. 1-53.*

Lortie, D. "The Partial Professionalization of Elementary Teaching." In Sieber and Wilder, 1973, op. cit., pp. 315-25.

Lortie, D.C. *Schoolteacher: A Sociological Study.* Chicago: University of Chicago Press, 1975.

Rosenthal, A. "Pedagogues and Power." In Sieber and Wilder, 1973, op. cit., pp. 353-60.

Sarason, S.B. *The Culture of the School and the Problem of Change.* Boston: Allyn and Bacon, 1971. See especially "The Teacher: The Role and Its Dilemmas," pp. 151-73, and "The Teacher: Constitutional Issues in the Classroom," pp. 174-94.

IV. School and Community

Charters, W.W., Jr. "Social Class Analysis and the Control of Public Education." In Useem and Useem, 1974, op. cit., pp. 98-114.

Clark, B.R. "Interorganizational Patterns in Education." In Brinkerhoff and Kunz, 1972, op. cit., pp. 356-66.*

Corwin, R.G. "The School in its Power Environment." In *A Sociology of Education: Emerging Patterns of Class, Status and Power in the Public Schools.* New York: Appleton-Century-Crofts, 1965, pp. 343-90.

Corwin, R.G. "The School's Responses to its Power Environment." In *A Sociology of Education*, Ibid., pp. 391-417.

Crain, R.L., and Street, D. "School Desegregation and School Decision-Making." In Sieber and Wilder, 1973, op. cit., pp. 401-11.

Fantini, M., Gittell, M., and Magat, R. "Local School Governance." In Useem and Useem, 1974, op. cit., pp. 86-97.

Fein, L.J. "Community Schools and Social Theory: The Limits of Universalism." In Sieber and Wilder, 1973, op. cit., pp. 412-24.

Fuchs, E. "Pickets at the Gates." In *Pickets at the Gates: Two Case Studies.* New York: Free Press, 1966, pp. 3-59.

Fuchs, E. "School Boycott: Education in the Streets." In *Pickets at the Gates*, Ibid., pp. 63-200.

Herriott, R.E., and Hodgkins, B.J. "The Environment of American Educational Systems." In *The Environment of Schooling: Formal Education as an Open Social System.* Englewood Cliffs, N.J.: Prentice-Hall, 1973, pp. 32-60.*

Iannaccone, L., and Cistone, P.J. *The Politics of Education.* Eugene, Ore.: University of Oregon, 1974.

Kerr, N.D. "The School Board as an Agency of Legitimation." In Sieber and Wilder, 1973, op. cit., pp.380-400.*

Litwak, E., and Meyer, H.J. "The School and the Family: Linking Organizations and External Primary Groups." In Sieber and Wilder, 1973, op. cit., pp. 425-35.

Peterson, P.E. "The Politics of American Education." In Keslinger and Carroll, 1974, op. cit., pp. 296-347.

Sjoberg, G., Brymer, R., and Farris, B. "Bureaucracy and the Lower Class." *Sociology and Social Research* 50 (1966): 325-37.*

Tumin, M. *Social Stratification: The Forms and Functions of Inequality.* Englewood Cliffs, N.J.: Prentice-Hall, 1967.

Wayland, S. "Structural Features of American Education as Basic Factors in Innovation." In M. Miles, ed. *Innovations in Education.* New York: Teachers College Press, 1964, pp. 587-613.*

Wirt, F.M., and Kirst, M.W. "The Local Conversion Process: Boards and Subsystems." In *The Political Web of American Schools.* Boston: Little, Brown, 1972, pp. 78-95.*

Ziegler, H., and Peak. W. "The Political Functions of the Educational System." In Useem and Useem, 1974, op. cit., pp. 47-59.

V. Other Perspectives

Coser, L., ed. *Sociology Through Literature: An Introductory Reader.* Englewood Cliffs, N.J.: Prentice-Hall, 1963.

Goffman, E. *Behavior in Public Places.* New York: Free Press, 1963.

Heggen, T. *Mr. Roberts.* Boston: Houghton Mifflin.

Kaufman, B. *Up the Down Staircase.* Englewood Cliffs, N.J.: Prentice-Hall, 1965.

Parkinson, C.N. *Parkinson's Law.* Boston: Houghton Mifflin, 1957.

Peter, L.J. *The Peter Principle.* New York: Bantam, 1969.

Potter, S. *One Upmanship.* New York: Holt, 1952.

Reisman, D. *The Lonely Crowd.* Garden City, N.Y.: Anchor-Doubleday, 1955.

Townsend, R.C. *Up The Organization.* New York: Fawcett World Library, 1971.

Wilson, S. *The Man in the Gray Flannel Suit.* New York: Simon and Schuster, 1955.

Wouk, H. *The Caine Mutiny.* Garden City, N.Y.: Doubleday, 1951.